SUSTAINABLE COMPETITIVE ADVANTAGE AND THE AMERICAN DREAM

How Business Can Create the First and Save the Second

Jim Olson and Bob Bennett

Copyright © 2013 Jim Olson and Bob Bennett.

All rights reserved. No part of this book may be reproduced, stored, or transmitted by any means—whether auditory, graphic, mechanical, or electronic—without written permission of both publisher and author, except in the case of brief excwrpts used in critical articles and reviews. Unautorized reproduction of any part of this work is illegal and is punishable by lew.

Note: The stars on the cover represent the 12 states whose representatives signed the U.S. Constitution on September 17, 1787.

ISBN: 978-1-4834-0029-7 (sc)
ISBN: 978-1-4834-0028-0 (e)

Because of the dynamic nature of the Internet, any web addresses or links contained in this book may have changed since publication and may no longer be valid. The views expressed in this work are solely those of the author and do not necessarily reflect the views of the publisher, and the publisher hereby disclaims any responsibility for them.

Any people depicted in stock imagery provided by Thinkstock are models, and such images are being used for illustrative purposes only.
Certain stock imagery © Thinkstock.

Lulu Publishing Services rev. date: 04/12/2013

Acknowledgments

Jim Olson

Thanks to my wife for encouragement, my students for curiosity, Dean Roger Weikle for opportunity, Dr. Keith Benson for feedback, and my co-author for his expertise in Toyota operational management methods.

Bob Bennett

To my loving and patient wife who makes life worth living;
To my son who shares my passion for Lean
Management and makes me proud;
To the many colleagues from whom I continue to learn so much;
And to Jim Olson for allowing me to
contribute to his excellent book.
Thank you!

TABLE OF CONTENTS

Preface ix
Introduction xi

The Roots of Free Enterprise 1
Management Defined 3
Planning.. 5
Organizing...33
Leading 53
Controlling 67
Hoshin Kanri Putting Your Management Tools to Work 73
An Opportunity Lost 129
The Fifth Input 131
Conclusion 141
A Glossary of Hoshin Kanri Terms, Tools and Techniques 145
Books That Provided Illumination 151
End Notes 153

PREFACE

Jim Olson

Soon after I retired from a 35-year career in the auto industry, I was named the Executive in Residence at Winthrop University's College of Business Administration in Rock Hill, South Carolina. Part of my duties included teaching a management course. While it adequately covered the core theories, I thought the 700-page textbook lacked real-world flavor and perspective. To supplement it, I wrote *The Little Red Box of Management Tools*—a collection of management practices I learned at Ford and Toyota. Some of its content—updated and compressed—reappears in the following pages. But this book has a different audience and purpose.

This time, the audience is businesspeople who want to improve themselves and their companies by learning how Toyota creates Sustainable Competitive Advantage at the individual and corporate levels. The primary purpose is to dig deep into Toyota's lean management methods. Wielding the shovel is long-time friend and newly added co-author Bob Bennett. Like me, Bob is a Toyota retiree. Unlike me, he is an expert in Hoshin Kanri—the operational tools, techniques, and processes underlying Toyota's impressive capabilities. Bob helped lead Toyota's massive North American expansion in the 1980s and 90s. Today he heads Lean Consulting Associates LLC, which helps corporate clients around the world learn and apply Toyota methods.

Over the years since we retired, Bob has invited me to contribute some of my time to his company, but I could never see a way to help. Finally, during a visit he and his wife JoAnn made to our South Carolina home a few years ago, we decided to combine our nearly 50 years of Toyota experience in a book his clients would find useful. When the economy and our national politics continued to deteriorate, I expanded the project's focus to also address those frustrated by the tepid economic recovery, partisan political paralysis, and growing public distrust of both business and government.

I was prompted to do so by a parallel I noticed between public- and private-sector governance that suggested a possible process for tackling the problems. For 76 years, Toyota's founding precepts have provided the "center" supporting the company's competitive advantage. For 225 years, the U.S. Constitution has fulfilled the same function for America. Both of these management systems have been effective because they are constant at the core, adaptive at the margin, and based on the unchanging roots of human motivation.

Every time Toyota strays from its strong center, it stumbles into a self-inflicted crisis (in addition to those caused by earthquakes, exchange-rate shifts, and other events beyond the company's control). America too has begun to stumble from crisis to crisis as the Constitution has been subverted and evaded to alter government's chief domestic purpose from assuring equal opportunity to providing equal outcomes.

Now we risk the possible destruction of America's unique can-do combination of opportunity, responsibility and hard work that has provided an example for the world to envy and emulate. I believe the American dream can be saved by America's business people. A small part of this book's purpose is to urge them to lead the rescue.

Introduction

My college days never hinted that I'd end up teaching. In 1964, I graduated with a BA in English literature from Stanford University. Then—courtesy of the US Navy—I learned my first management lessons. A master's degree in journalism from Northwestern University—funded by my wife's labor and the GI bill—led to a job in Public Affairs at Ford Motor Company where over 16 years I rose to mid-level management. Then in 1985 Toyota called.

The Japanese juggernaut, as U.S. news media later dubbed it, was about to begin expanding in North America. Worried about potential public and political backlash, Toyota wanted an experienced American to form an external affairs division including government relations, public relations, product publicity, philanthropy, corporate social responsibility, and later, shareholder relations and corporate advertising. The assignment was to defend Toyota's interests and develop relations with stakeholders who would publicly and politically support the company's growth in North America. Oversight of Toyota's small-but-growing U.S. motorsports program was an additional inducement to leave gray, dysfunctional Detroit for sunny Los Angeles and the learning opportunity of a lifetime.

The precepts that define Toyota's policies and practices were first stated at its founding 76 years ago. Although the words have evolved, the essential substance has not changed. At its core, the "Toyota Way" stresses customer satisfaction, respect for people, continuous improvement, hatred of waste, and love of challenge. Toyota people are expected to:

- Be humble, courteous and cooperative
- Hate waste, revere efficiency, and strive to create value
- Recognize customers as the company's most important stakeholders
- Respect individual creativity, but use the collaborative power of teamwork
- Realize that perfection is *never* possible, but improvement *always* is
- Go and see because true understanding requires firsthand experience rather than secondhand reports
- Seek opportunities, pursue excellence, and challenge competitors
- Embrace the responsibilities of citizenship wherever Toyota does business
- And always maintain a margin of safety in case of a potential downside.

The "learning" corporate culture these principles have forged is disciplined, ethical, focused on excellence, constant at its core, adaptive at its margin, and hyper competitive. It also is risk averse—rarely taking a bold action until the way forward is thoroughly analyzed and contingency plans prepared.

Toyota is not perfect. The causes of its occasional stumbles also lurk in the company's otherwise admirable culture. But I was amazed by the depth and breadth of Toyota's analysis and planning compared with the lack of it at my previous employer. It wasn't until I started teaching that I realized what a wonderful management model Toyota had provided me to use in the classroom.

I arrived at Toyota as the company reached a historic turning point. Although it was Japan's biggest company and the world's fifth-largest automaker, Toyota still was largely a national firm, serving most of its major overseas markets with products made in Japan. But the massive build-up that would make it one of the world's biggest automakers and a very large presence in many overseas markets was beginning. As a cultural and political facilitator in what would become Toyota's biggest market, I was ideally placed to observe the lean and disciplined management methods that make the company such a powerful competitor.

Whether you are CEO of a traditional company with a recognizable organization chart and full-time employees or head of a virtual enterprise that directly owns nothing but desire, ideas and a reputation, most of the principles defining what you do, why you do it, and how you go about it are the same and the tools and techniques similar. Your goal is to create a useful and attractive product or service then make money by so delighting customers that it will be very difficult for competitors to steal them. That's why the tools described in this book apply to all businesses—large and small, bricks or clicks.

At Toyota, I learned that these sensible tools must be based on ethics and integrity that build stakeholder trust and support. They also must stress the collaborative creation of genuine value; evolve slowly; be supported by long-term, disciplined application; and be deeply embedded in a company's corporate culture.

At the best companies, the culture is the "leader" and management's primary task is to preserve it, keep it relevant to the competitive situation, and assure that everyone in the company understands and abides by it. Companies are primarily people, processes and culture. *The third tells the first how to do the second.* If the culture is not both eternal and adaptive, success will be fleeting because there will be no consistent self-image and behavior to make the company unique and its business model won't evolve with the changing environment.

Strengthening and evolving the culture has become even more important in today's flatter, more horizontal organizations. As power and leadership are decentralized and more broadly distributed, culture and training—not direct, day-to-day managerial supervision—must guide the individual daily decisions and actions that create the company's reputation and lead to long-term success.

For example, as Toyota rapidly expanded its global operations, hiring thousands of new employees worldwide over a decade, the top managers in Japan tried to assure that all members of the company clear around the world fully understood and practiced the "Toyota Way"—a difficult teaching and training challenge only partially achieved.

I also learned that effective management tools form an interlinked system that must be applied in a holistic and balanced way to be fully successful. A couple of pirated techniques planted in an inefficient and ineffective corporate culture will not support lasting success. Firms trying to quickly copy the Toyota Production System (TPS) without fully comprehending its deep organizational roots soon learned this lesson.

THE ROOTS OF FREE ENTERPRISE

CAPITALISM AND THE CONSTITUTION

Here in America, management theory and practice have evolved within a free-enterprise economy built on a laissez-faire foundation guaranteed by a unique national governance system. This is no accident, but rather the result of careful planning by some visionary rebels more than two centuries ago.

During the summer of 1787, 55 delegates representing 12 states (Rhode Island abstained) gathered in Philadelphia to establish a federal government and create a constitution to control it. They knew that man is not perfectible and utopia is not possible. Having just won a war of independence from tyranny, they also knew that the best government is small, limited, economical and accountable to the people who create it. They designed a constitution to maximize the likelihood that America's government would be all of these things. On September 17, thirty-nine of them signed it on behalf of 12 states represented by the stars on the cover of this book.

The founders cleverly structured America's management system to simultaneously free and harness man's self-interest to a double duty—the creation of individual wealth and the promotion of the general welfare. By guaranteeing the right of the individual to pursue personal benefit (the "pursuit of happiness" described in the Declaration of Independence whose key component they viewed as the right to own private property) with minimal government interference, they freed the marketplace to create the wealth to found enterprises and fund jobs that would support an unprecedented living standard.

This unique partnership between a *limited* government and a *free* market self-regulated by supply and demand made America the most productive and powerful nation in history—a position now at risk.

MANAGEMENT DEFINED

Value-Creation Chain

In: Money, Material, Morality, Manpower, Information

Design — Produce — Market — Sell — Service

Out: CDV (Customer Defined Value)

Planning, Leading, Organizing, Controlling, Kaizen ⟶ SCA (Sustainable Competitive Advantage)

Management is planning, organizing, leading and controlling money, material, morality, manpower and information to produce Customer Defined Value (CDV). If this value-creation process (carried out by cross-functional teams that unite primary corporate functions such as design, production, marketing, sales and service) is executed efficiently and effectively using the Plan Do Check Act (PDCA) process, it yields continuous improvement (kaizen) and profit. These methods can eventually create Sustainable Competitive Advantage (SCA)—the ultimate state all businesses strive to achieve.

The persistently urgent PDCA process has been around for decades under this name and in other forms. Some of the forms go way back. For example, one of the most successful coaches ever, John Wooden, used a form of PDCA to go 40 years without a losing season and lead the UCLA basketball team to 7 consecutive national titles. He first wrote down his personal "continuous improvement" methods in 1934, two years before Toyota Motor Corporation—which has helped popularize similar management methods—was founded. Winning was not Wooden's primary goal. He recruited the best players he could and focused all his effort on assuring that each of them played to his full potential. Winning was the primary byproduct.

In his 1917 book *Industrial Management,* French expert Henri Fayol included only four inputs into management (money, manpower, material and information). In view of today's demands, I have specifically added morality to Fayol's four. His definition dictated the format of my first book *The Little Red Box*—a red, steel toolbox with four empty drawers labeled "Planning," "Organizing," "Leading," and "Controlling" which I then filled with tools.

Planning

Creating Your Future Before Someone Else Does

> "If you know neither the enemy nor yourself, you will lose every battle."
> Sun Tzu *On The Art of War*

As the famous Chinese military strategist Sun Tzu noted, knowledge of your capabilities, your competitor's capabilities, and the situation are vital to success. You might say that luck favors planning and preparation. Centuries later, the most successful football coach ever, Notre Dame's Knute Rockne, supplemented the Chinese general: "The secret of genius is an infinite capacity for taking pains."[i]

There are few better examples of this insight than the 1879 battle of Isandlwana in what is now South Africa. It pitted approximately 4,000 highly trained British troops (plus a few thousand local farmers) armed with expertise, arrogance, and long-range Martini-Henry rifles against 20,000 wily Zulus armed with courage, spears, and cowhide shields. Because of their modern firepower and previous successes, the British expected to win the battle despite the nearly five to one numerical advantage enjoyed by the Zulus.

However, due to overconfidence and under-preparation, the British were outmaneuvered. In addition, their ammunition was packed in tin-lined, steel-strapped cases requiring a special tool to open. Oops! Someone misplaced most of the tools. Largely ignorant of the local geography and unable to get enough ammunition quickly enough, the British were outmaneuvered and overwhelmed. The majority of them were slaughtered—including most of the officers who made invalid assumptions and took insufficient pains. What's the primary lesson for business? It's always management's fault [ii]

Three additional underlying lessons also are evident:

1. Never underestimate a competitor.
2. Always overdo your preparations.
3. Pay constant and close attention to the field of battle.

These lessons are the heart of good belt-and-suspenders corporate planning, which I call *what keeps you on your feet when life pulls the rug out from under them*. Good managers, particularly those who have climbed well up the corporate ladder, have learned to be conscientious, conservative, skeptical, and nimble. In fact, conservatism and "taking pains" are primary hallmarks of the planning process used by management at successful corporations. Let's look at how many of them go about it.

The ideal planning process starts with a corporate-wide communication loop designed to harvest expertise and insight, forge shared understanding, create organizational alignment, and build employee commitment and excitement.

Like most other corporate processes, planning begins at the top and flows downhill. But then, if done properly, it defies gravity and flows back uphill. This is because a successful communication loop always ends where it began: (1) sender encodes and sends message; (2) receiver decodes message and sends feedback conveying understanding or seeking clarification; (3) sender and receiver repeat this loop until shared understanding is achieved.

This communication process takes place inside a particular corporate culture created by core ideology ("Who are we?") and core purpose ("What are we here to do?"). The answers to these questions form the company DNA, which determines its corporate culture. Like a star on the horizon, this DNA evolves very slowly, if at all. It sets the company's direction by telling everyone inside how to make and take the hundreds of daily decisions and actions that define the company, create its reputation, and build (or destroy) its brand strength. It is a big, self-centering gyroscope that you hope is exactly mimicked by a little gyroscope inside each employee. Together, big and little keep the company balanced and on course.

Core ideology need not be spelled out. For example, when you visit the corporate campus of athletic equipment manufacturer Nike there is no big, blinking sign saying "Core Ideology Here →." Instead, the photos of winning athletes all over the place graphically scream that the company culture is something like, "We enable victory."

Such a clear and passionate ideological statement can be useful in recruiting the best and brightest. Management expert Peter Drucker called the best and brightest "volunteers" because they can work anywhere. This also supports my conclusion that effective core ideology is aimed primarily *in*, not *out*. Its chief purpose is to inspire, focus and motivate employees, not to differentiate the company from competitors—although it often does both.

Successful companies with strong and ethical core ideologies tend to have a *stakeholder*, rather than a *shareholder*, philosophy that includes some commitment to make a useful contribution to society.

Although maximizing shareholder wealth is important, most employees will not sacrifice their hearts, souls, and free time to add a dollar per share to the bottom line. But research has demonstrated that many of them will commit all three if they believe they are creating value for themselves and society as well as the company. Later in this book, I explore some other effects of a stakeholder versus shareholder approach to business.

The planning process begins with a leader's "vision." Imagine that you are the leader. To find your vision, you ask yourself and your executive team four foundation questions:

1. *What* is our product or service?
2. *Who* will buy it?
3. *What* do they want in the product, sales and service experiences?
4. *How* can we give it to them in ways that will energize us, separate us from competitors, capture customer loyalty, create profit, and build sustainable competitive advantage?

Values ("What do we hold most dear?"), *vision* ("Where are we going?") and *strategy* ("How will we get there?") result from answering these basic questions in detail. Eventually, the information and analysis gathered to fully answer the questions and arrive at choices are assembled into the company's business plan.

Once this groundwork is complete, a mission statement ("Why we are here.") is generated to capture and communicate corporate purpose, provide direction, and ignite excitement and commitment. If it's expressed well and communicated persuasively, this lightning in a bottle can help to focus and fuel employee performance. Unfortunately, many mission statements are "group think" products that try to say too much, spreading employee focus across too many unclear goals. Here are a few examples.

Cisco

"Cisco solutions provide competitive advantage to our customers through more efficient and timely exchange of information, which in turn leads to cost savings, process efficiencies, and closer relationships with customers, prospects, business partners, suppliers, and employees." [iii]

I'll bet this statement was constructed by a room full of bright people during a professionally facilitated off-site meeting followed by golf, tennis, drinking, dinner, guest speaker, and more drinking.

Translation: "Cisco is the people network. We build our customers' competitive edge by enabling them to more efficiently and effectively share information with their customers, employees, and business partners."

This version is more economical, if not very inspiring. The first sentence is lifted from Cisco's advertising. What's the lesson? If the advertising agency defines corporate purpose better than the planning department, go with the flow.

Walmart

"We work for you. We think of ourselves as buyers for our customers, and we apply our considerable strengths to get the best value for you. We've built Walmart by acting on behalf of our customers, and that concept continues to propel us. We're working hard to make our customers' shopping easy." [iv]

Translation: **"We help our customers live better by offering top value at low prices every day."**

A good mission statement should set bold goals while capturing and communicating corporate purpose in order to ignite, fuel and focus employee action.

To do so, it must be short, simple, sincere, and—if possible—inspiring.

Closing the Loop

By hammering out Values, Vision, Strategy and Mission (VVSM), you and your executive team have defined purpose and path. But you still don't have a plan. To get one, you must establish specific goals; determine, assign and allocate the three R's (Responsibility, Resources, and required Results); establish timetables; and amplify strategy with detailed tactics. For that, you need help from the people who will carry out the plan.

So you communicate the VVSM to everyone in the company and ask them to promptly answer three questions in as much detail as they can: 1) How would you improve these ideas? 2) What specific supporting goals and plans would you establish in your area of responsibility? 3) What resources (budget, people, time, etc.) would you need to achieve them?

To answer these questions, the organization usually employs basic planning techniques such as SWOT analysis (Strength, Weakness, Opportunity, Threat):

(1) What are our **S**trengths?
(2) What are our **W**eaknesses?
(3) What current **O**pportunities in the outside environment can we take advantage of?
(4) What current **T**hreats in the outside environment do we need to defend against?

The information generated by SWOT and other analysis provides specific goals; KPI's (Key Performance Indicators) for defining and measuring success—more about this later; resource requests; timetables; suggested roles; and—in some cases—suggested structure. All of this is fed back upstream to top management. With the communication loop completed, management finalizes the plan and directs the organization to implement it.

This planning loop harvests suggested improvements from the organization's collective brain, begins the process of unifying everyone behind the plan by making them feel they own it, and starts to generate the necessary excitement to achieve its goals.

Corporate Social Responsibility and the Triple Bottom Line

Public demands that business work to improve society as well as make a profit stem from America's protestant roots. Over the past thirty years or so, this demand has acquired even more insistence and a formal name. Corporate social responsibility (CSR) requires a company to maximize its positive and minimize its negative impact on society. Like all other business factors, a CSR strategy must be thoroughly defined and included in the company's business plan. Today, many companies react to continuously growing CSR expectations by reporting results to a triple bottom line—profit, people, planet—at the end of each fiscal year. Note that the first CSR responsibility "*p*" is profit, without which a company cannot survive to fulfill the other two. As Drucker noted, "To do good, you must first do well." [v]

I helped set up Toyota's US philanthropy programs and oversaw them for many years. Most of our investments supported education, particularly if a program had a twist that also would help strengthen the company's environmental reputation.

We benchmarked other large companies to assure that Toyota was among the leaders with a similar focus. We also issued a report annually describing our CSR programs and progress. And finally, we used public opinion research to carefully monitor the growth of CSR expectations and periodically reacted with new programs to increase our philanthropy and further reduce the environmental impact of our US facilities and products. This "monitor-and-move" strategy is standard operating procedure at most observant companies.

Jim Olson and Bob Bennett

Benchmarking, Converging, and Commoditizing

Let's consider the benefits and drawbacks of a technique called benchmarking. It has become fairly standard practice for companies to visit and examine other companies—both inside and outside their industry or market segment—to see if they can pick up ideas for improving their own operations. Even Toyota, an acknowledged leader in product development and manufacturing, uses benchmarking from time to time and also has been quite open about letting other companies—including other automakers—tour its facilities.

While observing many of Toyota's visitors over the years, my co-author noted that too many did not approach benchmarking with the proper "learning" attitude. Failing to park their corporate ego at the door, they focused on areas where their company led rather than gleaning potential improvements from areas where they lagged. Or they simply didn't focus—much of the group falling behind and making small talk instead of keeping up and asking how and why Toyota did things the way we did.

If you benchmark simply to measure your performance against a Best In Class (BIC) company, you will miss the most important potential gain—finding out how the company does it so you can adopt or adapt its methods to improve your own. What good did it do visitors to discover that Toyota's equipment uptime was 25 percent higher than theirs, that our workers were up to 50 percent more productive, that our warranty costs per unit were half theirs, that our service parts fill rate was 6 percentage points higher, and that our inventory turn rate was double? Knowing the height of the cliff won't enable you to climb it if you don't see the handholds marking the route to the top.

Bob also frequently observed significant shortcomings in their grasp of Toyota's business processes. Visitors could easily see the "tools" of the Toyota Production System (TPS): kanbans, andon cords, standardized work processes, quality circles, visual management and cleanliness. But without some diligent digging, they could not see the Toyota Way, the "culture" in which the tools are rooted; the Purpose/Process/People PDCA system and the thinking, values, methods and practices that integrate the visible tools into an invisible, closely aligned enterprise-wide management system that continuously builds organizational learning and competitive advantage.

Despite its potential for improving performance, benchmarking does have drawbacks. Harvard's Michael Porter has observed an unfortunate side effect he calls "competitive convergence."[vi] As competitors more frequently and intensely study and copy one another's methods, their approaches and techniques tend to become similar, which can lead to equality that erodes product uniqueness, undercutting brand strength and customer loyalty. This denies companies the ability to charge a premium that can be invested in improvement. As competing companies pursue productivity and market share in the same segments, combined production capacity can outrun demand (you usually think of the other companies' plants as the excess) and their products can become "commoditized"—interchangeable with one another in customers' minds.

Customers love this because it enables them to demand higher content and quality at a lower price. But it can slowly bankrupt companies. Witness what has happened in the North American steel, airline, and auto industries where market and economic pressure have forced downsizing, merger, and bankruptcy.

Plans Emerge; Bracketing

At this point, the process has produced a plan—or, more precisely, three plans: best-case, likely, and worst-case. Prudent companies usually "bracket" by at least partially constructing the bookend plans on either side of the most likely scenario in an attempt to capture all possible "futures." Later, I'll describe the "what-if" game that drives the bracketing process.

Typically, a company implements the likely case while putting the best—and worst-case scenarios on the shelf in case they are needed. Some go even further by constructing "crisis management" plans for specific potential scenarios. As the scientist Louis Pasteur said, "Chance favors only the prepared mind." [vii]

One Plant Too Many: Toyota Over-reaches?

Most conservative companies rarely execute their best-case plan because it can cause them to over-reach and become vulnerable to sudden, unexpected changes in circumstances. I believe Toyota violated this safeguard beginning in the late 90s by switching its primary focus from *better* to *bigger* and building too many plants in too many countries too fast.

Here in North America, the tipping point was the decision to enter the full-sized truck market and construct a billion-dollar plant in Texas to fuel the effort. The plant has frequently been underutilized because gas prices rose, the economy shrank, truck sales sank and buyers of Detroit's trucks proved more loyal than Toyota anticipated. Underutilized production assets like the Texas plant, adverse economic conditions, earthquakes, a tsunami, and the yen's strong exchange rate all combined to cause Toyota to lose money for the first time in 57 years.

Unfortunately, I was part of the American management team that helped convince the Toyota Motor Corporation (TMC) board to build the truck plant. When you become an officer of a TMC subsidiary, you no longer just oversee several departments. You join a group of executives charged with responsibility for the success of the entire subsidiary. This requires a different mindset and a broader approach—*a responsibility I mostly ignored*. Instead, I viewed the Texas plant from the 50-foot perspective of the guy overseeing government relations. To me, it represented more American employees and a big economic contribution in a politically potent state, all of which could increase Toyota's influence.

Instead, I should have taken a 5,000-foot officer's perspective and posed the "what-if" questions top managers at successful companies should always ask. This can require you to deny the natural human "herd" instinct by highlighting risks your colleagues may not want to acknowledge.

I also believe TMC was receptive to the truck-plant proposal because an attitude change was underway at our parent company. Within even very good companies there can lurk a "dark side"—confidence that can bloom into arrogant over-reach when fertilized by success and public praise.

I have learned that pride has two close neighbors—one good and one bad. On its right is competitive spirit, which can generate enthusiasm that improves organizational performance. But on its left is hubris that seduces management into looking in the mirror instead of out the window.

Certain of its capabilities and lured by the prospect of becoming global number one, I believe Toyota overreached—outrunning its supply of fully experienced human resources. The dilution of Toyota's capabilities with new employees not fully trained in the Toyota Way hampered the company's ability to achieve swift growth while also cutting costs and protecting the high product quality that had long been its chief brand strength.

The result was a record number of reputation-shredding recalls encompassing nearly nine million vehicles worldwide over an eight-month period plus the biggest fines ever levied against an automaker by the U.S. National Highway Traffic Safety Administration (NHTSA).

Recalls by all automakers are likely to grow in size and frequency for two reasons: 1) They share a highly stressed and shrinking supplier base 2) Most of them also employ nearly continuous cost-cutting, which (among other things) sharply increases the components shared among their vehicles, driving up the numbers covered by each recall. Although cost savings generated by the gains in economy of scale fatten their bottom lines, they become more vulnerable to widespread quality failures that can undermine public trust in their products.

At the root of Toyota's situation lay some out-of-date management structure, a shortage of experienced resources, and internal distrust that slowed decision-making. To stop its bleeding, Toyota needed to slow its rate of growth, rekindle its leadership in product quality, and change its structure to improve reaction speed and accuracy—particularly in crisis situations. These shortcomings are being addressed by Toyota President Akio Toyoda as this book is published. The result should be a less insular, more agile company with a management structure that is more localized and empowered.

The situation also required the company to slow down and rebalance cost-cutting and product quality with renewed attention to the latter. In a marketplace where customers increasingly experience little difference in the traditional Things Gone Wrong (TGW) quality of a Toyota, a Honda or a Hyundai, Toyota also needed to further emphasize effective TGR (Things Gone Right) differentiators such as design, technology and vehicle dynamics. The automaker's most recent models show improvement in all these areas.

The company needs to continue digging out the internal distrust and flawed communication at the root of its crisis. Despite determined efforts to do so, Toyota was not able to sufficiently change its mindset, structure and governance processes as it grew from a national company serving overseas markets with Japan-built products into a company with large manufacturing operations all over the world. Instead of sufficiently training and fully empowering the non-Japanese managers of its growing overseas subsidiaries, the company continued to make most of the important decisions affecting major markets in Japan and then directed regional management to implement them.

Centralizing decision-making in Japan separated it from execution carried out overseas, slowing both and often producing decisions that were insufficiently sensitive to local culture. It also hampered communication, planning, cross-training and executive development among the company's regional operations and sent an unfortunate message—"We don't fully trust you"—to many of Toyota's non-Japanese managers. This produced an insular culture not sufficiently "globalized" to lead the company into the next century and beyond.

As noted, Toyota has recently moved to correct these structural and cultural problems with more decentralization and localization of power in its major overseas subsidiaries. But there still may be disagreement on basic strategy lurking within Toyota. The company's founding precepts have always stressed a stakeholder philosophy with the customer at the head of the line. It appears that most of the top management still holds this viewpoint. But concurrent with its strategic shift to bigger rather than better, another contingent of top executives supported a shareholder philosophy. Toyota does not have enough resources to battle itself as well as competitors. Abraham Lincoln's observation "A house divided against itself cannot stand" applies. Toyota must resolve any remaining strategic division and stay on one pathway going forward.

Because of its basic integrity and immense capability, I believe Toyota always will find ways to protect its reputation. Its growing sales and regained #1 position among the world's automakers are positive signs that customer trust is returning. Meanwhile, the company is learning that leading the parade allows everyone following to take a clear shot at the bull's eye pinned to your backside.

The Tortoise and the Hare

VVSM, SWOT, benchmarking, bracketing, and what-if comprise the basic process that leads to a final and fully resourced corporate plan. But *change is the only constant*, so you're not done yet. In fact, planning is an endless process requiring continuous observation and adjustment. A competitor launches a new and disruptive technology that partially or completely obsoletes your product. A key supplier goes out of business. Your core customers age, forcing you to modify your product to meet their changing capabilities. The birthrate spikes, delivering another "pig-in-a-python" generation to work its way through the market, surprising you with new tastes, challenges, and opportunities. A trade agreement opens new markets overseas. The economy dips into recession. Raw material prices accelerate. Your cost of capital increases as interest rates rise or your credit rating falls. You get hammered by a sudden, major shift in an exchange rate.

These ever-changing factors and many more force planners to continually re-assess the environment and the basic assumptions supporting the company's business model. Always keep in mind that drawing a conclusion and only then seeking facts to support it is the way of someone ruled by ideology not reality or more concerned with *appearing* right than *being* right. It can lead only to failure. Always start with facts.

Based on the results of this perpetual paranoia, you adjust the organization to the new terrain and re-implement the plan for another trip. The key considerations are to be observant, open to new ideas, and to *always run scared*.

In addition, you must be ruthless about waste. You can't always solve tomorrow's problems with yesterday's solutions. Instead you must destroy the no longer productive, retrieve the rescued resources, and invest them in creating tomorrow. Companies that forget this need for what Austrian economist Joseph Schumpeter called "creative destruction" become big, slow and saddled with overblown, out-of-date structure—frequently ending up as corporate road kill.

For example, consider the thirty companies that currently comprise the Dow Jones Industrial Average. Started in 1889 by the editors of *The Wall Street Journal,* the Dow's purpose was to capture a representative mix of US companies that could be used to track the general health of American business. Only four of the thirty companies that constituted the Dow in 1929 remain part of the index today (AT&T, DuPont, GE, and Proctor & Gamble). As it sank toward bankruptcy, GM was replaced by Cisco. [viii] The rest have changed their name, been bought by some other firm, or gone out of business. As noted business book author Jim Collins puts it, "They have fallen from great to good to gone." [ix]

Most companies go through the reassessment exercise that keeps them alive, on track, and relevant at least once a year when annual results become available and the budget and plan for the coming fiscal year are constructed. In volatile markets and industries, the process can be virtually continuous. As I noted earlier, it is called Plan Do Check Act (PDCA). You plan, execute the plan, check the results against your goals, improve the plan to reduce the gap, and begin again. If you're successful, this never-ending cycle generates continuous improvement—a powerful "tortoise" that can steadily inch competitors to death.

This classic planning process is logical, conservative, and risk-averse. If carried out in a disciplined fashion, it might eventually reach the ultimate goal of all corporations: sustainable competitive advantage. However, in order to attain the goal, it's likely that occasionally, you will have to add a leaping "hare" to the race: a big hairy audacious goal (BHAG). Think of the tortoise as discipline and the hare as creativity. Successful companies learn to balance the two forces, using more of one or the other in order to react to changes in the environment.

A BHAG is a long-term (ten-to-fifteen-year) goal. BHAG's usually come from someone in top management who is truly visionary rather than just strategic or tactical. And they are, of course, the primary product of entrepreneurs. Here are a few examples.

"I will build a motor car for the great multitude . . . It will be priced so low that any man making a good salary will be able to afford it . . . When I'm through, everybody will have one, the horse will have disappeared from our highways, the automobile will be taken for granted, and a large number of men will be employed at good wages."
Henry Ford when he founded Ford Motor Company [x]

"We will build a car for every purse and purpose."
Chairman Alfred Sloan describing GM's income/life-stage collection of vehicles from Chevrolet to Cadillac—a disruptive new business model that nearly broke Ford [xi]

"I want twice the fuel economy of a comparable car with an internal-combustion engine."
Then Toyota President Hiroshi Okuda as he increased the fuel-efficiency goal in the middle of developing the gas-electric Prius, which proved to be a huge competitive advantage for Toyota. [xii]

Successful BHAGs are frequently disruptive, usually seize first-mover advantage, and always create corporate capabilities that are difficult, if not impossible, for competitors to copy (the primary element of sustainable competitive advantage). They are the "hare" to the PDCA "tortoise."

At leading companies like Toyota, the capability-creating process generated by a BHAG is continuous and routine, not occasional. Called Hoshin Kanri, it is fully described later in this book.

Everyone on the Same Page

All levels of the plan (corporate, divisional, departmental, team, and even individual) must be linked, driven by the same strategy and focused on the same goals. This way, the entire corporate workforce is pulling on the same rope in the same direction. As we'll see in a later chapter, when managers sit down with their people to map out the year ahead, the corporate plan should be in front of them so that each individual's goals can be structured to help achieve departmental, divisional, and corporate goals.

No Man is an Island

Because of its lean management methods and enterprise-wide coordination, at Toyota this deceptively simple part of the annual planning process is much more complex—typically taking about three months and a lot of collaborative effort. Here's why.

First, the annual plan is done under the umbrella of a mid-range plan (3-5 years) that identifies specific large enhancements to the company's capabilities that will be necessary to support the unfolding business strategy.

Second, Toyota managers realize that annual performance improvement objectives can be achieved only by eliminating faults in the company's value-creation processes that block them from reaching the next higher level of capability.

Third, virtually all important processes creating and delivering value to internal and external customers flow horizontally into, through and out of the company from suppliers to distributors and other business partners in the "extended enterprise." Since virtually all meaningful improvement in these shared value-creation processes require collaboration, input, support, schedule coordination, and resources prioritization among the company and its allies in the extended enterprise, each manager's annual plan of process improvement projects must be developed in collaboration with the managers of each supporting department within the company and usually within business partners as well. The needs of these "internal customers" must play a big part in his planning.

Consequently, the targeted improvement is no longer just a simple individual or departmental goal, but must instead be treated as part of an extended matrix of improvement that has to move forward as a whole.

Limited resources, challenging objectives, and conflicting priorities assure that several face-to-face meetings will be required to resolve issues and obtain signed commitments of support from each manager in the value-creation chain. These commitments and the intensive preparation leading up to them greatly enhance smooth execution by creating shared understanding and buy-in before execution begins.

This is in stark contrast to dysfunctional organizations that plan briefly, fail to link departments, exclude extended enterprise partners, and execute badly with "cooperation" that resembles civil war.

The World in Your Face
Planning in a Global Environment

No matter whether you are a CEO or a team leader, planning is getting harder because the game is continually expanding, the rules of engagement are becoming ever more complex, and there are more and more players. There's no longer any place to hide. For example, just because you decide not to market overseas doesn't mean foreign competitors won't get right in your face here at home.

In theory, you engage today's global environment at two points: an inner and an outer ring. The inner ring, the "task" environment, is where your customers, employees, suppliers, distributors, and competitors co-exist, clash, and cooperate. Here, you can put your hands on events and have some control over inputs and outcomes.

The outer ring, however, is composed of economic, sociocultural, technological, demographic, political, legal, and regulatory forces over which your company alone cannot exert much influence, but which can hugely impact your business. All you can do is detect these forces coming over the horizon and attempt to exploit or survive them as best you can.

The Inner Ring
Suppliers and Distributors

If you are a manufacturer, two of the most important entities in your task environment are your suppliers and your distributors. The former partially control your product cost and quality by what they provide and the latter partially determine your reputation by the attitude they project. You literally are the bologna in the sandwich.

Companies with a shareholder focus often view themselves as first among equals and—when under economic pressure—will beat down supplier and distributor profit margins to protect the quarterly earnings, stock price and dividends shareholders value—as well as the executive bonuses tied to these factors. Treating suppliers and distributors as lesser beings is short-term thinking that degrades their ability to provide the support you need to succeed over the long term. Managers with this sort of approach also might take other ill-advised actions such as decreasing the research and development budget—mortgaging tomorrow's capabilities in order to feed today's bottom line. If they are in charge for a long time, they can destroy a company.

By contrast, companies with a stakeholder mentality realize that a value chain (supplier → manufacturer → distributor → customer) is simply a coalition of stakeholders cooperating to collectively transform resources into customer satisfaction and then share the mutually created wealth. They realize that they cannot succeed if their business partners do not succeed as well and therefore subscribe to the commandment written by novelist Alexandre Dumas, "All for one and one for all." [xiii]

Shareholder Versus Stakeholder

Treating companies providing your input and companies selling your output as truly equal business partners collaborating with you to create value and gain wealth *together*, is an approach often used by successful companies with long-term viewpoints.

An example would be Toyota and Honda helping their suppliers to increase their quality and decrease their cost instead of—as GM, Ford, and Chrysler have so often done in the past—arbitrarily demanding a price cut regardless of the impact on the supplier. Incidentally, the Detroit Three have recently realized the wisdom of adopting this "value-sharing" practice in their supplier relations.

Dealing with Competitors

Your competitors—other companies that provide the same product or service or could do so—also are part of your task environment. Strong competitive rivalry improves quality and technology. Imagine what the product quality of GM, Ford, and Chrysler would be today if Honda, Nissan, and Toyota and several European automakers had not stuck a competitive spur into them.

But, as noted above, competitive rivalry can commoditize products, degrade prices, lower profits, and create mutually assured destruction. Before this stage is reached, it's logical for companies to find ways (industry coalitions, cooperative pre-competitive research, pooled sourcing, or joint-venture manufacturing) to cooperate in cost-reduction and product-enhancement activities.

Cooperation also can provide pooled financial strength and the magnified political influence necessary to overcome heavy capital investment requirements or government regulations that undercut competitive capability. Note, however, that this sort of cooperation requires the participants to completely understand and respect antitrust laws and be willing to be relatively honest and open with one another—not easy feats.

The Outer Ring
Economic, Technology, Sociocultural, and Demographic Forces

Other than behaving ethically and contacting your congressmen and senators, there is very little you can do to keep the Fed from raising interest rates or inflating the currency to keep the economy from recession, or to prevent Congress from passing ever-more onerous business regulations. These are examples of forces over which your company alone can exert little or no control. Unless you unite with other companies—a need I'll discuss near the end of this book. But you can prepare your company to deal with the likely consequences. For example:

- Minimize debt and maximize retained earnings so your company has pockets deep enough to survive today's recession without jeopardizing its ability to ride tomorrow's rebound. *The Economist* noted that DuPont invested heavily in R&D during the Great Depression of the 1930s and succeeded during the post-depression boom because 40 percent of its

products (including world-changing nylon and synthetic rubber) were less than ten years old. [xiv]
- Create new technology or track its development by suppliers so that you are better prepared to incorporate it into your products as Toyota and Honda did with the computer technology enabling reliable gas-electric drive-trains.
- Track your current customers and realize that age is making their eyes weaker, their bodies less flexible, their fingers stiffer, and their reactions slower, requiring you to accommodate their changed capabilities and needs with incremental product improvement even as you chase the next generation of younger consumers with innovation.
- Monitor major-market population projections to discover where around the globe you must invest in new manufacturing or distribution capability over the coming decades.
- Track political developments in international trade and have what-if plans ready to implement when a new trade agreement presents opportunities.

As any race driver knows, the current corner's exit is the launch ramp for the next straightaway. If you routinely employ these conservative measures, when a downturn arrives you will have the resources to outspend, out-invent, outlast, outsmart and out-accelerate less-prepared competitors. You will be able to rocket into the next upturn, gaining brand strength, market share and profit that will enable you to repeat the strategy during the next downturn. Retained earnings, a top-tier credit rating, and prudent preparation can help build a powerful and sustainable competitive advantage.

Planning Tools

So, what tools do we put into the toolbox "Planning" drawer?

- Corporate Culture (DNA): The star on the horizon that defines and guides a company, composed of core ideology (Who are we?), core purpose (Why do we exist?), and the answers to several other questions that follow.
- The four foundation questions begin the planning process: 1) What is our product or service? 2) Who will buy it? 3) What do they want? 4) How can we give it to them in ways that . . . ?
- Values: What do we hold most dear?
- Vision: Where are we going?
- Strategy: How will we get there?
- Mission: Why are we here? Best answered with a succinct, inspiring statement designed to fill employees with urgent purpose and point them in the same direction.
- Goals: Targets that comprise the focus of the company's strategy. They must be clearly defined before success can be achieved and measured with key performance indicators (KPIs), which will be discussed in following sections of this book.
- The planning loop: The corporate-wide communication process that directs Values, Vision, Strategy, Mission (VVSM) *down* the corporate hierarchy and asks for suggested improvements, tactics, timetables, and resource projections to come back *up*. This "loop" creates shared understanding and ownership of the plan from top to bottom and aligns, commits and energizes the organization to execute it.
- SWOT: Classical analysis technique composed of four questions: 1) What are our strengths? 2) What are our

weaknesses? 3) What opportunities are available in the business environment? 4) What threats face us?
- The three Rs: Responsibilities, Resources, and required Results; in order to create and achieve a corporate plan, you *define the first, grant the second, and demand the third.*
- Benchmarking: Examining other companies to see what useful improvements you can adopt or adapt.
- Bracketing: The planning practice of composing 1) best-case, 2) likely-case, and 3) worst-case plans so that the company is relatively ready for all envisioned "futures." Most companies routinely implement the likely case.
- Crisis Planning: Establishing a standing crisis committee, anticipating various potential incidents, and constructing fairly detailed "just-in-case" plans for each so that the company is prepared to react quickly if one of the scenarios suddenly comes crashing through the boardroom wall.
- Commoditizing: A destructive process resulting from intense competition. It erodes product uniqueness, making your products interchangeable with competitors' products in customers' minds and denying producers the opportunity to differentiate themselves and their offerings from one another. The usual result is overproduction, falling prices, and failing companies that chase the same customers with increasingly similar products and processes. But the customers are happy. Avoid it by building brand strength that can help create sustainable competitive advantage (easy to say but hard to do).
- Linkage: Assuring that plans at all levels in the company (corporate, division, department, team, individual) are linked and aimed at the same goals, causing everyone to pull on the same rope in the same direction.
- PDCA (plan, do, check, act): Plan it, do it, check results against objectives, improve the process to narrow the gap, and then do it over and over and over to achieve . . .

- Kaizen: The powerfully competitive "tortoise" of *continuous improvement*, which combined with . . .
- BHAG: A *big hairy audacious goal* that creates new corporate capability can achieve . . .
- Sustainable Competitive Advantage: A unique combination of vision, strategy, and capabilities difficult, if not impossible, to copy—consigning competitors to second place.
- Run Scared: What the British troops at Isandlwana did not do but what smart, well-managed companies always do. Any plan these companies decide to execute has a built-in margin of safety.
- Certainty: What planners—and all managers—long for but always lack (and what government should always try to create). Time, cost, and capability limit information-gathering activities. Consequently, you will never have *perfect knowledge* before you must decide among competing courses of action. In fact, many issues allow you time to find only a small patch of likelihood in a swamp of uncertainty before requiring you to stand and decide. Good planning can minimize risk, but eventually the pressure of circumstances will push you into placing a carefully considered bet.
- Feelings and Facts: The two "F" words. Good planners tend to downplay the first and embrace the second. Our second president, John Adams, called facts "stubborn things."[xv] Another bright politician, the late U.S Senator from New York, Daniel Patrick Moynihan, said, "You are entitled to your own opinions, but not your own facts."[xvi] Feelings are both unavoidable and vital. Ongoing brain research clearly demonstrates that our emotions affect every action we take, helping to shape and drive both personal and corporate decisions. They are absolutely necessary to honesty, integrity, ethics, and authentic, connected leadership—particularly during a crisis. But facts are where intelligent people can

most easily find the day-to-day common ground necessary to agree on a course of action. *Facts* drive the planning that precedes decision-making. *Find them, analyze them, use them.*

- At Toyota, Genchi-genbutsu (go personally to the actual place and see the problem yourself) is perhaps the most important aspect of this fact-finding process. When a problem is reported, Toyota people rush to it, observe it, and ask questions to deeply probe and understand its character and causes and assess its likely impacts. In addition to gathering facts and data, they also translate feelings into usable facts. Not their own feelings, but the feelings of the customer disappointed by the defect, the salesman or service technician struggling to fix it, or the worker forced to use equipment ill-suited to manufacturing the product without the defect. Accurately captured and succinctly reported, these feelings help fuel the scientific method of problem solving that enables Toyota to develop and test hypotheses to confirm the effectiveness of potential solutions.
- The planner's mind: Good planners are inquisitive, fact-driven, aware of their limitations, skeptical and paranoid. They start most days with the same two questions: "What has changed?" and "What are the short- and long-term implications of the change?" Even if they are not familiar with it, they also believe in the command summarized by *genchi-genbutsu* because *firsthand* experience always tops *secondhand* reports.

All of these characteristics coalesce in an ability to perceive patterns, opportunities, and threats in ambiguous and sometimes contradictory information. When you combine the planner's mentality, these tools, and disciplined operational techniques designed to constantly harvest wasted resources for re-investment in value creation, you have a very powerful management system. But we need to add one final tool.

A Lesson from General Motors

The final tool in the planning drawer is the what-if game. What better place to determine the need for this vital tool than General Motors. As we began writing this book, GM—once America's biggest company—had slid into bankruptcy while my management students tracked its glide path. As I have for several years now, I had divided them into teams and asked each team to prepare and deliver a fifteen-minute power point presentation answering these questions:

1. Using the principles taught in this course, explain how GM went wrong and identify the "root" cause for its unfolding failure.
2. Can GM recover? What measures would you recommend to restore it to fully competitive condition?
3. Was it wise for the government to bail out GM?

Although they have identified and described many symptoms and suggested some good remedies over the years, only a few of my student teams have fully captured the root cause of GM's downfall: *a proud, powerful and unimaginative corporate culture that prevented management from asking, "What if?" and then taking timely and aggressive action to change the company's future.*

GM celebrated its hundredth birthday in 2008. During its first 60 years, it became America's biggest company and the world's biggest automaker. But then the rules of competition that had enabled its success began to change. Even as the membership of US labor unions fell, their demands continued to rise. Foreign-owned competitors established productive, lower-cost, non-union operations in the "right-to-work" states of the southern US and their high-quality fuel-efficient products—particularly cars—became very popular. While GM's market share slowly shrank, successive generations of management failed to ask the right questions and take sufficiently aggressive actions:

- What if competitors offer products that are lower-cost and higher-quality than ours? For a long time, GM was blind to this even as it was happening.
- What if they continue to establish North American manufacturing operations that are more productive, lower-cost, and more flexible than ours?
- What if we end up with too many unprofitable or marginally profitable dealers unable to represent us properly and virtually impossible to get rid of?
- What if eight different brands stretch our resources too far, forcing us to turn out increasingly generic products differentiated only by their nameplates and not supported by sufficient marketing resources?
- What if the cost of overly generous medical and retirement benefits we have granted in a vain effort to buy labor peace make each vehicle we build significantly more expensive to manufacture than similar foreign-nameplate products?
- What if global demand for oil drastically accelerates, driving the price of gas up and buyers out of trucks and SUVs? (Note that this is the key question my colleagues and I should have asked as we considered recommending the Texas truck plant to the Toyota board of directors.)
- What if our foreign competitors succeed with the fuel-efficient, gas-electric "hybrid" technology we rejected?
- What if we get deeply into debt, a sudden financial crisis restricts credit, and a sales crash chokes off our cash flow?

While most of these circumstances materialized slowly, a more curious and fact-driven corporate culture would have noted the trends and reacted much more quickly and aggressively with measures that prevented it from slowly painting itself into a corner. A less insular culture also might have been more open to life-saving change.

Organizing

Elephants Can't Dance

Successful companies realize that change is the only constant and they can succeed only by continuously destroying no longer useful parts of their past and recycling the rescued resources into a better future.

The ideal corporate structure to match this reality would be a single cell that automatically adjusts its shape to changing circumstances, transforming itself swiftly and effectively no matter where it is touched. Unfortunately, no one has yet figured out how to create such a perfectly adaptive organization. Instead, being human, we tend to do the opposite. Longing for stability, we try to deny change and impose order by categorizing and filing everything—including each other.

In many corporations, for example, we house people doing similar jobs in little towers, wire each tower with a clear chain of command, and provide rules telling everyone what to expect and what is expected of them. Then we stack all the little towers up into a multi-tiered pyramid with an expensive, all-powerful CEO standing on top like the wee wax groom on a wedding cake, pointing toward *his* true north and bellowing, "Follow me!" We need a quick, intelligent amoeba. But—left to our instincts—we create a lumbering elephant. *And elephants can't dance!*

This sort of corporate structure is inflexible, slow to react, and resistant to change. Like a large oak tree with too many branches and too few roots, it projects size and strength but doesn't have sufficient foundation to stand up to the winds of change. Unfortunately, at least some of it also is necessary. However, tools and techniques we will discuss can make it more efficient, effective, and rapidly reactive to marketplace pull and competitive challenge.

But first let's review. Remember the four basic foundation questions from the previous chapter:

1. What is our product or service?
2. Who will buy it?
3. What do they want in the product, sales, and service process?
4. How can we give it to them in ways that will energize us, differentiate us from competitors, capture customer loyalty, make money, and build sustainable competitive advantage?

Continuously finding customers, satisfying their desires (even those they don't yet know they have) and building lasting, profitable relationships with them are the basic goals of all business. The way an organization is structured and motivated can help or hamper efforts to do so.

A certain amount of structure is necessary, but—like government—less is best. Here's why. In addition to being centralized, traditional corporate structure tends to be *vertical*. Grouping people with similar skills and functions into departments makes it easier for them to work with and learn from one another <u>inside</u> their department and for managers to oversee their activities. But like the tide, the market's pull is horizontal, requiring these different departmental silos to overcome the *insularity of similarity* and link their activities in order to provide what customers want when, where, and how they want it. Successful companies have learned to react to the horizontal tug of the market quickly, efficiently, and accurately. How do they do it?

Think of market demand as a series of ropes. A customer demands something by tugging on one end of a rope. The retailer on the rope's other end feels the tug with his left hand and, in turn, tugs on the rope in his right hand, connecting him to you, the producer. You feel the tug with your left hand and tug on the ropes in your right hand, connecting you to your first-tier suppliers. They, in turn, tug on the ropes connecting them to their suppliers. Except for the customer, everyone in this demand chain tugs only when tugged upon and production begins only when the customer-initiated tug reaches the far end (tier-two suppliers) of the chain.

No company ever fully achieves this idealized *just-in-time* pull system. Many factors can kink the ropes. But, as we'll see in the section on "Controlling," even compromised versions can drastically reduce the waste and expense of stockpiling "*just-in-case*" resources within the system by activating production in response to genuine customer "pull," not in response to the cost-driven "push" exerted by expensive and underutilized manufacturing capacity.

In a traditionally structured company, the departmental silos with their layered verticality create a series of walls that can create friction that slows or blocks response to this horizontal tugging. The cost of creating, staffing, and maintaining the silos also tempts companies to book a profit by producing and pushing inventory and cost onto retailers, regardless of true final-customer demand.

In addition to being expensive, these silos also can force *communication* and *decision-making* into a vertical, up-and-down pattern centered on top management. This slows the company's reactions to both market demand and competitive challenge.

But as business has gone global, competition hyper, and communication electronic, corporate structure has been forced to evolve to meet the constantly increasing need for faster, more accurate reaction to the outside environment and to overcome the growing challenge of constantly improving competitors—in short, to more efficiently and effectively deal with the expanding and evolving tugs of the business environment.

However, management still needs to see over the walls and be seen by employees in order to control, coordinate, unify, and lead. Furthermore, the expertise, experience, and skills housed in the departmental silos need to be effectively brought to bear on the company's customer-service processes to assure quality, improve productivity, enforce consistency, and control costs.

Creating a structure that allows control, collaboration, and quick reaction to customers and competitors to smoothly mesh rather than clash is a balancing act. Furthermore, it's different for each company and each set of circumstances. And finally, the structure must continuously evolve in step with the external environment, which crosses new borders every day. Wow, it's global, three-dimensional chess—a game you can win only by creating a *learning* organization able to:

- Adapt quickly to the changing external environment
- Foster creative collaboration, clear communication, and quick, accurate decision-making
- Coordinate and focus "silo" expertise to satisfy customers more efficiently and effectively than competitors
- Continuously create new corporate skills to cope with challenge and change
- And react rapidly and consistently no matter where demand tugs on it.

As we will see, the primary tools to achieve this are goal-setting, teamwork, control/motivational systems, corporate culture and leadership.

Note that structure might be different at various points in the organization in order to meet different needs. Once size and type does not fit all needs. For example, production activities might require structure intolerant of mistakes and waste in order to assure quality and enforce cost control. But the same "justify-the-cost" approach would smother a research and development department needing to explore likely opportunities that can turn out to be expensive blind alleys. As I already noted, balancing discipline and creativity is one of the key functions of good management.

Furthermore, a company might go through organizational phases. As it grows from local to regional to national to international to global, it might evolve from a product setup with structure devoted to each product line, for example, to a setup with structure devoted to all business within a certain geographical area such as North America or Europe. This regional setup describes Toyota today, but it began as a national company that initially served its overseas markets with Japan-built products.

Or a conglomerate might adopt a company-within-a-company approach where individual divisions dedicated to each type of business regularly report results to a small central "corporate" staff that sets goals, tracks performance, and enforces cost control, market focus, and a uniform culture.

Continually advancing computer technology (data gathering/storage/analysis, swift/broad sharing of information, and instant-global-24/7 communication) has facilitated the development of flat, flexible, reactive "learning" organizations with geographically dispersed operations. But thinner control structure—fewer managers with broader spans of control—and more expansive access to actionable information also empower employees, requiring a new framework and rigorous training to guide their decision-making when close, day-to-day supervision is no longer possible.

Companies Come in All Sizes

Because of my background, I have focused on the organizational practices and pitfalls of large corporations. But there are many more small companies than large. How do you organize your own business?

Among the smaller forms you can use before resorting to a full corporation are a sole proprietorship, a partnership, a limited liability company, and an S corporation. Which one you pick depends on your desired combination of privacy, flexibility, tax benefits, and shielding against personal liability for company debts.

For example, a sole proprietorship has only one stockholder (you) with all the privacy and flexibility that implies. But you pay personal tax on the company's profits, and your personal assets can be seized to pay off company liabilities. In a limited liability company, you can have an unlimited number of shareholders, the tax benefits are similar to a partnership, and your personal assets are shielded from company liability.

You might start your company as a sole proprietorship and evolve into one of the other forms over time. But large or small, you still will need to hire the best people you can afford, minimize cost, and create a strong "compass" culture as your company grows beyond your ability to run it in a personal, hands-on fashion.

Growth Requires Culture Creation and Training

Well-known restaurateur Danny Meyer faced these imperatives when his company grew beyond the very successful Union Square Café into a company with hundreds of employees working at 11 successful New York City eating establishments. How do you extend success beyond your small start without expanding into bankruptcy? Meyer puts it this way. "I managed by example, and I had yet to learn how critically important it is to lead by teaching, setting priorities, and holding people accountable." [xvii]

In other words, when you can no longer always be there to directly monitor, control and assure performance by saying, "Watch and do what I do," you need goals, operating procedures, a clear and compelling corporate culture, and training to do it for you. And that means you will have to create structure to set the goals, train your people, assure follow-up, and reward high performance.

Designing Effective Structure

Whether it's a small or large company, part of your managerial function will be job design—dividing tasks into specific jobs that will best achieve organizational goals by simplifying, enlarging, or enriching responsibility. Another part will be designing structure to group employees with similar functions and responsibilities into departments and then figuring out how to breach the walls between the departments to create the cross-organizational communication and collaboration that satisfies customers.

As stated above, departmental benefits include learning from others doing similar jobs and ease of monitoring and control for management. But unintended consequences can include the silo effect that scrambles communication, slows decision-making, inhibits interdepartmental cooperation, and blocks sight of the big corporate picture.

The usual solution is cross-departmental teams composed of members who bring expertise from their departmental or divisional "silos" to the team table. These teams focus on satisfying the "pull" of customer demand to achieve corporate goals. For example, most automakers assure the effective focusing of silo expertise (sales, product development, chassis engineering, body engineering, engine engineering, manufacturing, etc.) on meeting market pull by using cross-functional product teams.

When I was working at Toyota North America, the management of the Camry team consisted of a Japanese chief engineer, an American executive engineer, a manufacturing engineer, and a product planner from the sales department who represented customer needs and desires. When a new Camry was introduced, the team members were immediately out in the market, assessing acceptance and picking up reaction from dealers and customers to feed into the next Camry, the planning of which started immediately.

Teamwork

Why are teams effective? Because they have *more* of everything than someone working alone: more brains, more resources, more knowledge of the pieces and parts of the organization, more understanding of the marketplace, and more diversity of viewpoint. They link the collective, collaborative, creative brainpower of the various silos and focus it to satisfy customers and achieve organizational goals. They also enable employees to feel they are part of something bigger than themselves, which increases job satisfaction. But teams will do all of this only if they are managed properly. Here are some suggestions. When forming and managing a team:

- Pick busy people because they know how to get things done.
- Make sure each team has a full deck of cards by picking people with complementary skills.
- Keep teams relatively small—no more than seven to nine members so that no one can hide from individual responsibility and discussion and decisions are more easily conducted and reached. When necessary, supplement with temporary members who leave when their particular task is done.
- Reward both individual and team performance with, for example, a two-bonus system. (You get what you reward.)
- Clearly link team goals to corporate objectives, give members the training and tools they need, set a date for final results, and get out of the way.

- Monitor and lead from a distance with a light hand, stepping in to coach—not command—or provide more resources when necessary.

When you are a team member:

- Organize the meetings yourself if you have to, but never hold one without an agenda and some advance preparation by participants. To do so usually invites a time-wasting bull session disguised as "brain-storming."
- Check your ego at the door, but make sure everyone's team role and responsibilities are clearly understood and try to assure that everyone's viewpoint is heard and respected. Some Toyota people call this approach the "Three C" system: Consideration, Communication, and Cooperation.
- Try to keep discussion moving on track. Politely interrupt "dominators" and ask non-participants what they think. Get all the viewpoints out on the table for discussion.
- Be the last to offer ideas so you have the benefit of everyone else's. Then sum up: "Let me see if I understood everyone's ideas . . ." This enables you to summarize and state the meeting's outcome, a powerful role.

Teamwork is a way to breach the walls and bridge the gaps; but traditional structure still is necessary, and it needs to be clear and easily understandable. Each organization requires a chain of command, specifying each manager's relative authority (the power to hold people responsible for their actions and to decide how and when organizational resources are used) and the span of that authority (how many departments report to each manager).

Traditional structures were tall with many levels of authority and narrow spans of control. As noted above, this slowed decision-making by separating it from execution and forcing it upward in the organization. It also was bloated and expensive. Thankfully, this sort of structure is quickly disappearing today. To gain speed and market reactivity, corporate structures tend to be lean with fewer and wider levels that combine decision-making and execution rather than separating them. Decisions above designated levels of cost, complexity or importance are still reserved for top management. This sort of empowerment can decentralize and diffuse control, possibly diluting shared focus and unity of purpose. Broad spans of control also can overload and burn out managers responsible for them.

In addition to accountability, the answer is a strong, clear, positive corporate culture and lots of training so that every employee knows how to make decisions that fully reflect the company's values, mission, vision, strategy and goals. Assuring the propagation and continuous improvement of this sort of learning, collaborative, "compass" culture during periods of swift international growth can be difficult, a problem Toyota has faced for years.

One way to avoid creating expensive structure (particularly important in cyclical industries where structure added during booms drags during busts) is to use strategic alliances in which two or more firms share technology development or jointly own and operate a production venture. Taken to its extreme, this approach yields a "virtual" company that owns nothing, instead out-sourcing all its activities to free-standing entities, which it coordinates.

How to Run What You Have Built

Running the structure you have built is no different than any other business process. You begin and continue with questions. For example:

- Have we selected the right goals?
- Is our process and product quality higher than competitors'?

- Are we measuring success properly?
- Are we turning inputs into outputs efficiently and controlling our costs?
- Are we encouraging innovation or simply incentivizing mediocrity?
- Are we making enough money to continually reinvest in increasing our competitive edge?

Depending on the answers you get, apply controls to alter the outcomes. The controls can be:

- Feed-forward which anticipate and try to prevent problems
- Concurrent which correct problems as they arise
- Feedback which assess results—with a customer satisfaction survey, for example—and guide corrective measures.

In any case, you must pay close attention to how you define success because, as management expert Peter Drucker said, "What gets measured gets done." [xviii]

So measure the right things the right way.

As we'll see, your managers must participate in this definition process because the selected measurements become the Key Performance Indicators (KPIs) they must meet. You compare their results to the mutually selected goals and quantify the gap. Then you coach them to decide what corrective actions will narrow or close it. These could include less difficult KPI's, more training, better tools, a different approach, more investment, a different structure, more effort, or a different person.

You also must be careful to provide some flexibility in goal-setting and KPI creation. If you set the bar too high or maintain goals that become unrealistic because external circumstances have deteriorated, employees might cheat to meet or quit to escape them. This is another reason for always keeping one eye cocked out the window to watch the competitive and market situation.

And you must focus on the desired time horizon. For example, if you want steady, long-term gain in market share, you would not want to curtail R & D investment in order to fatten short-term profits.

Drucker called this goal-setting process Management By Objectives (MBO). You sit down with your direct reports one at a time just before the company's next fiscal year to review their achievements and agree on their individual goals for the coming year. You meet with them periodically during the year to discuss progress. At year end, you base their merit raises, bonuses, and promotions on performance against the mutually agreed goals. As Drucker might have said, "You get the performance you reward."

As discussed in the planning section, the resulting *evolutionary* change or kaizen is part of the PDCA process in which feedback controls provide the information to construct feed-forward controls, completing the never-ending cycle driving continuous improvement. If you do it in a disciplined way, over time, you create a learning, continuously evolving organization that stays in step with the changing marketplace so you never have to blow it up and start over.

In his chapter on Toyota's operational management methods, my co-author will explain why MBO methods fall short of today's competitive needs.

Starting Over

But what if you become part of an undisciplined company that has failed to pursue continuous improvement or made unrealistic long-term commitments it cannot keep? It might then become necessary to resort to *revolutionary* change, which has been compared to changing all four tires while the car is going seventy miles an hour.

Crises can take many forms. Frequently, they seem to explode suddenly into existence. Most appear to result from an operational failure. But if you dig deeply enough, you are likely to find that the hidden root cause of most crises is really a cultural failure that has been growing for some time (often years). Usually, it is failure to consistently use PDCA to adapt or failure to play the what-if game that enables a company to avoid forging cast-iron commitments that limit adaptation and result in adverse long-term consequences.

Whether slowly developing or suddenly arising, most crisis situations require revolutionary change that is rapid, bold, and dramatic. They might require you to fire people, outsource work, and sell assets. It's likely that they will require the quick development of new ways of doing things. This requires a strong, charismatic "transformative" leader who can convince stakeholders that big, swift changes are required and effectively communicate a persuasive and inspiring vision of what—with drastic, quick, coordinated effort—the organization can become.

Revolutionary change will use many elements of the standard planning process already described. But usually, too little attention is given to the persuasive leadership skills required to convince people to change.

Leaders in a PDCA company subtly exercise low-key control from the back row in the form of observation, support, coaching, and questioning. This sort of fact-driven approach is the core of effective managing. But in times of crisis, it must be combined with vision and passionate, authentic, emotional communication that will break through the complacent "business-as-usual" attitude to force the quick, gut-wrenching changes that will enable the company to survive. This requires a leader who can combine the rational and the emotional in an inspiring "come-with-me-to-the-mountaintop" pitch that connects; exactly the sort of leadership GM lacked when its final crisis crashed into the boardroom.

But let's be clear. Too often, the need for emotional communication and rapid, disruptive change is created by bad management practices. The purpose of *revolutionary* change is to restore an organization to a state where *evolutionary* change can be reinstated. If the proper PDCA methods—and the continuous, disciplined, incremental improvement they create—had been diligently used to begin with, a revolution might not be necessary. *The continuous improvement produced by sound, conservative corporate planning, and disciplined execution is the firmest possible foundation for long-term business success.*

Recruitment
Inside, Outside, or Outsourced?

When you have an opening, you can fill it by hiring from outside or promoting from inside. Considering both sources provides a broader pool of candidates. An outsider can provide a fresh viewpoint, give you the opportunity to increase the diversity of your workforce, or add new skills to the company's capabilities. But the downside is ignorance of your organization that requires time and training to rectify. You also are likely to be more certain of an insider's capabilities. But by far the most important benefit of promoting from within is the positive message it sends to your people: "Work hard and you will progress."

If you hire outsiders, pay particular attention to their "fit" with the corporate culture. Skills and knowledge can be taught, but personal chemistry resists change. Many companies use psychological tests to weed out candidates who can't work well in a team environment. Some companies even have members of the team with the opening conduct the candidate interviewing, testing, and hiring.

However, be careful not to unconsciously create a homogenous organization that lacks the diversity of culture, viewpoint, and experience you need to achieve creativity and improve market knowledge and connection. Consider the change-resistant cultures, trouble and turbulence of companies like Ford and IBM with influential founding families or GM with a long-serving, culture-creating leader like Alfred Sloan who was President and then

Chairman for an astounding 33 years. These days, diversity is a recruitment goal of most smart and successful companies.

Proctor & Gamble relies on promoting from within and has a very complete system for tracking high-performance employees and assuring that they get the broad experience necessary to climb the corporate ladder to a leadership position. That's why former chairman A.G. Lafley is confident that the P&G "bench" will deliver fully developed replacements for today's top managers when they retire.[xix] Recent news media reports, however, indicate that even P&G may be stumbling under the leadership of Lafley's successor.

Other options include outsourcing the work or hiring a temporary employee. Both provide more flexibility than hiring a full-time employee. Both also avoid or reduce the overhead cost of benefits, which usually add at least 30 percent to a position's salary. And temporary employees provide a safety valve that can enable a company to lay off workers during a downturn in the economy.

You should routinely consider these options in order to minimize structure. The final option is not filling the position. When an opening occurs, always ask whether the position adds enough value to justify refilling it or whether you could partial out its activities to other positions and use the freed-up resources elsewhere in the organization.

The over-riding consideration in recruitment is excellence. If you hire the very best raw material you can afford, provide proper training and motivation, and have a bit of luck, you'll win more often than you lose.

Retention/Training/Development

As I noted, Peter Drucker said the best employees are volunteers because they can get a job anywhere. He also pointed out that sustainably successful companies tend to treat employees as an asset, not a cost. What is the link?

If you treat employees (or team members as many companies now call them) as a cost, a safety valve to be used in booms and abused in busts, you are unlikely to create the trust, teamwork, commitment, and excellence that form the foundation of long-term success. Instead, it's likely that you will generate cynicism, mediocrity, and high workforce turnover.

What you really want to do is *hire* and *keep* the best. How do successful companies do this?

- First, they offer competitive benefits and wages. You cannot recruit the best unless your basic package is at least equal to the industry average. That's why HR departments closely monitor economic conditions and other companies' actions.
- Second, they offer greater rewards (bonuses, stock, etc.) if the company does exceptionally well. They base the rewards on both individual and team value added, not time served. Former GE Chairman Jack Welch insisted that, if you don't reward your top performers well, regardless of seniority, you'll lose them. Remember, they're volunteers. Some companies use a double-bonus system to reward both individual and team performance. Incidentally, the benefit of a bonus is that it is one-time and does not permanently increase the company's labor costs by becoming part of base pay as would a merit raise.
- Third, they offer training, development, and opportunity for advancement; and they very systematically develop the next generation of leaders. GE and P&G have been superb at this. Your best performers often are natural leaders and they eventually want to run something. If you don't give them a chance to do so, some other company will. Note that the traditional route of advancement has been to move up a rung on the organizational ladder. Today's flatter companies reduce the opportunity for this "climbing-the-ladder" path. Some companies address this problem by separating titles from pay

or creating almost-separate companies for different lines of business (a conglomerate arrangement) with "Presidents" in charge of each one.
- Fourth, they offer a feeling of belonging and self-fulfillment through achievement. In short, a satisfying place to work. As Abraham Maslow noted in his hierarchy of needs, this is a primary motivator for high-performing people.
- Fifth, they find what employees want and reward them with it. And they evolve the rewards to match the changing desires of succeeding generations.
- And finally, they always let you know how you are doing with timely and accurate performance feedback.

Motivating Performance

Work with your people to set their individual annual goals. Make them sign a "contract' stating their goals. Monitor performance using concrete Key Performance Indicators (KPIs) such as "sales" or "profits" if possible. Measure the gap between goals and results. Mutually devise and institute corrective measures. When the goals are achieved, raise them for the next cycle and do it all again. That's the essence of a PDCA-based performance appraisal system that will drive continuous improvement.

If the goals are difficult to quantify—for example "improve employee relations"—you might have to use trait or behavior appraisals. "Does this person exhibit leadership traits and behavior?" But keep in mind that this approach can be viewed as subjective, opening you and the company to a lawsuit if you downgrade or fire the person reviewed.

When conducting a performance review, always start with something positive. "I like what you have accomplished in this area . . ." Be as concrete as possible and use tactful, not harsh, language that focuses on improvement, not criticism. Express confidence in the employee's ability to improve and agree on a timetable for improvements to be achieved.

A considerable body of research asserting that this way of presenting performance reviews doesn't work has accumulated over the past few decades. Researchers say that an individual's need to suppress "cognitive dissonance" (inputs from the environment that disagree with and threaten your self-image) acts like a mental shield that rejects criticism. No matter how constructively and tactfully it is communicated, the individual will not change behavior. This is particularly true if the criticism comes from a superior.

In his recent book, *Management Rewired*, Charles Jacobson suggests that the solution to this impasse may already be evolving. Changing the source of the review from the manager to the individual's team mates appears to get around some of our mental shield. The team members, guided by the manager, select their own goals, decide team and individual rewards, and rate one another's performance. This discovery will continue the evolution of the manager's role from out-in-front, command-and-control alpha figure to a coach using Socratic questioning ("What do you think?") to subtly teach, inspire, guide, and support a team.

Research also is demonstrating that—after a certain level of pay is reached—money may sometimes no longer be the most effective motivator. Instead, something as simple as a free day once a month to work on a self-assigned business project may be a much more powerful reward.

Organizing Techniques and Tools

- Look in/look out; design your structure to suit your internal resources and the external environment. Then keep it up to date and always as simple, lean, flat, and adaptable as possible. Your

primary goal is to improve and accelerate your sensitivity and responsiveness to customers.
- Use cross-functional teams to link, coordinate, magnify, and focus "silo" power through diversity, collaboration, and synergy.
- Badly designed structure can smother initiative, leadership, and creativity, so make certain any structure you create encourages rather than discourages these important characteristics.
- Assure that managers have full control over the functions for which they are responsible and the necessary incentives and KPIs to motivate and measure performance. Don't stretch spans of control too far.
- As you decentralize and empower, reinforce the corporate "compass" culture to assure shared vision, focus, and consistency in decision-making. Also clarify responsibility and demand results. Without accountability, empowerment is likely to fail, not succeed.
- You need to increase walk-around, face-to-face contact because computers broaden and facilitate access to actionable information, diffusing power and decision-making throughout the organization. It's your job as a manager to make certain that distributed leadership actually achieves the company's goals, but don't smother initiative and learning by micro-managing. Individual problem-solving leads to learning, which strengthens the whole organization.
- Like bread dough, structure wants to rise and expand. Your people always want more people, so they can do more. They also believe that more people will increase their importance in the company. And they will try to reward their people with promotion, eventually fragmenting management spans and creating too much vertical structure housing more chiefs than braves.
- One of the problems with today's flatter, broader structures is that there are fewer levels to provide promotion opportunity.

Structure also is expensive, and it usually slows corporate reaction time. To avoid these consequences, force your people to focus on the essential, not the nice to have. Force them to convince you that any increase in structure will return more in customer value than it costs.

- Be stingy. Staff for the mean, not the extremes. You might miss some sales during peak demand, but you also may avoid laying people off when the business cycle bottoms out.
- If you properly develop your people, you will lose some of your best to competitors because you don't have enough leadership positions available. Get over it, keep in touch, and hire them back when you have an opportunity that fits. If you have led them properly, they will want to come home.

LEADING

LEADERSHIP REQUIRES FOLLOWERSHIP

A little research reveals as many leadership "models" as there are varieties of corn or cattle. Let's simplify by agreeing that there are two general forms of leading. "Pushing" works well in a learning company that uses cross-functional teams to continuously evolve and improve through PDCA. "Pulling" is best suited to a company in crisis requiring quick, revolutionary change to survive. Both styles are well described by Kolp and Rea in their book *Leading With Integrity*.

A pushing leader stands behind her people—coaching, encouraging, and providing tools, training and resources. She has a knack for turning abstract strategy into understandable tactics and the empathy to "read" people skillfully. In order to build their coping skills and assure that they get the credit when goals are achieved, the pushing leader empowers her people to deal with the particular situation and guides their efforts from the rear. She suggests rather than commands. Her favorite phrase is, "What do you think?" She listens carefully to your answer (which requires you to analyze the situation, create a plan of action, and explain it) and she rarely micromanages you. If you succeed, she applauds. If you fail, she asks "What did you learn?" All of these methods are employed at Toyota.

In contrast, the "pulling" leader works from the front. He is the very visible person on a white horse who emotionally communicates an inspiring vision of what the company can become and leads you out of the wilderness toward the vision. His favorite phrase is, "Follow me!" The most vital skills for this type of leader are insight, capability and authentic, inspirational, emotionally-based communication that convinces and unifies people. A pulling leader builds a vivid, visionary bridge from *is* to *can be* and inspires others to cross it with him. This is what any CEO charged with rescuing a failing company must do. No one will follow an unconvincing leader over the bridge. That's why strong, persuasive communication capability is an essential crisis leadership skill. Incidentally, neither of these two styles is gender-related.

General Dwight Eisenhower pragmatically described leadership as "getting the other fellow to do what you want him to when you want him to do it." [xx]There are few better examples of this knack than an incident during the Civil War described in *Killer Angels* by Michael Shaara. It occurred a few hours before the Battle of Gettysburg.

The central character was Union Army Colonel Joshua Chamberlain, definitely a "pulling" leader. He commanded the Maine 20th Regiment. At this point, he was a young, inexperienced officer who just a year or so before had been a professor at Maine's Bowdoin College. He was highly educated, fluent in several languages, and a powerful orator.

Chamberlain was ordered to accept 120 mutineers from the Maine 2nd Regiment who had unknowingly signed three-year contracts when most other members had signed two-year obligations. When the two-year militia men headed home, the three-year men mutinied because they weren't allowed to leave as well. Chamberlain's commanding general gave him three choices:

1) Convince them to fight
2) Take them into battle under guard
3) Execute them.

Even though he knew it was the riskiest option, Chamberlain chose strategy number one. When the mutineers arrived, he ordered the guards to unshackle them and leave. He called the mutineers "honorable men" who didn't need shackles and guards. Then he called for food and water for them and spent five minutes in his tent, listening to their spokesman, Sergeant Bucklin.

Only then did he stand in front of the mutineers to give the most important and persuasive speech of his young life. This is what he said:

> Bucklin has told me of your problem. I'll look into it as soon as possible. But there's nothing I can do today. We're moving out soon. We'll be marching all day and we may be in a big fight before nightfall. But I'll do what I can when I can.
>
> I've been ordered to take you with me. I've been told that—if you don't come—I can shoot you. Well, you know I won't do that. Not to Maine men. So that's that. But I've been ordered to take you along and that's what I'll do—under guard if necessary.
>
> You can have your rifles back if you want them. The whole Reb army is waiting for us up the road a ways and this is no time for an argument. I tell you this—we sure can use your help. We're down below half strength and we need you.
>
> I don't want to preach, but if you decide to fight alongside us, there are a few things I want you to know. This regiment was formed last fall back in Maine. There were a thousand of us then. There are not 300 of us now. But what remains is choice.
>
> Some of us volunteered to fight for the Union. Some came because we were bored at home and this looked like it might be fun. Some came because we were ashamed not to. Many came because it was the right thing to do.
>
> Most of us never saw a black man back home, but freedom is not just a word. This is a different kind of army. If you look at history, you'll see men fight for pay, for women, or some other

> kind of loot. They fight for land, or because the King makes them, or just because they like killing
>
> But we're here for something new. This hasn't happened much in the history of the world. We're an army going out to set other men free.

Bending down, Chamberlain grabbed a handful of dirt. Holding it up, he continued:

> This is free ground—all the way from here to the Pacific Ocean. No man has to bow. No man is born to royalty. Here, we judge you by what you do. Not by what your father was. Here you can be something.
>
> But this isn't about land—there's always more land. It's about the idea that we all have value. We're worth something more than dirt. I never saw dirt I'd die for and I'm not asking you to join us and fight for dirt. What we're all fighting for, in the end, is each other.
>
> If you come with us, I'll be personally grateful. But it's your decision. Now we have to move out.

All but six of the mutineers joined Chamberlain and fought at Gettysburg. His augmented regiment turned the tide of battle at a key point on Little Round Top, where the Confederate Army nearly broke through Union lines. During his years in the army, Chamberlain was wounded six times, rose to brigadier general, and was awarded the Congressional Medal of Honor for his bravery. After returning to civilian life, he became president of Bowdoin College and later in life was Governor of Maine. But I doubt he ever again gave such a pithy, powerful and pivotal speech. What leadership techniques did Chamberlain use to convince the mutineers to cross the bridge with him?

- He connected with them by calling them "honorable men of Maine" like himself and ordering the guards and shackles away.
- He demonstrated care by quickly supplying food and water.
- He began establishing trust by listening to their grievances, taking execution off the table, and promising support when the battle was over.
- He appealed to their pride and self-respect by saying he needed them.
- And he touched their patriotic emotion by showing them that the reason for fighting was nearly unique in history and something worth being part of.

Chamberlain was a charismatic communicator. He knew how to get out of <u>his</u> head and heart and into <u>theirs</u> in order to use their needs to make his goals their goals.

When you read some of the books dealing with leadership, you find that communication capability is accompanied by a blizzard of other "C" words, including character, caring, competence, conviction, consistency, courage, compassion, confidence, and charisma.

Whatever characteristics fuel it, leadership requires followership. To attract followers, I believe a leader must possess at least character, conviction, competence, courage and charisma—all of which must be used to achieve credibility and connection. Does he display honesty and integrity? Is her behavior guided by strong core values? Does he possess the necessary knowledge and skills for the task? Can she communicate her vision with the eloquence necessary to connect with and convince people that she is worth following? Does he walk his talk with an authenticity that creates credibility and trust?

Kolp and Rea insist that the primary leadership characteristics are character grounded in virtue, and competence gained from experience. As they put it, if a leader's character isn't virtuous, he won't do the right thing. If he's not competent, he won't do things right. Doing the right thing the right way at the right time is essential for a leader.

They go on to say that courage also is important because a leader lacking it will put his personal interests ahead of the organization and his people. Since your people closely watch everything you do, putting yourself first will inevitably undermine your credibility and their trust.

In other words, like nearly everything else in business, leadership is grounded in integrity, honesty and virtue that require you to put the best interests of the organization and your people ahead of your own. This is the best way to succeed over the long term.

How do you select the best course of action when faced by an ethical problem that presents several different potential solutions? Experts have built many different decision-making models to reach the right answer. I always found the "mom" test (Would my mother approve?) the most useful way to determine whether I was comfortable with a potential decision. Another effective way to test your comfort level is to imagine the decision described on the front page of the local newspaper with your name attached to it.

Negotiation

Sometimes, despite personal conviction and persuasive communication skills, you will encounter colleagues who want to follow a different path than the one you favor. You might have to use two important leadership skills to head off or minimize controversy that could undermine support for the necessary decision.

Negotiation can take two different paths to your desired result. Compromise *shares the pain* because everyone sacrifices something to the other participants. This approach assumes a fixed amount of resources that can be allocated differently, but can't be increased.

In contrast, collaboration assumes that resources can effectively be increased by using them more efficiently with a new, more productive approach jointly created by the participants during the negotiation. This way of tackling the problem *shares the gain.*

In facilitating negotiation, concentrate on the participants' needs, not their demands. Participants often lay out unrealistic demands simply to see if they can maximize their results. That's why you should concentrate on needs. Get all of them out on the table, find the common ground everyone can agree upon, move it to the "agreed" column, and concentrate negotiations on the remainder. Obviously, collaboration—rather than compromise—is the preferred approach.

Organizational Politics

You can greatly reduce the likelihood that your decisions will be challenged by making skillful use of organizational politics. As long as they are used to achieve organizational goals that benefit everyone instead of serving self-interest, political skills are ethical and can be very useful.

Immediately upon joining an organization, you should be looking for future leaders in your "class" with whom you can network and consult as you all rise in the corporation. You can depend upon this group of unpaid consultants for ideas and for support in the negotiations that are an integral part of business. In Japanese companies, the results of most negotiations often are decided outside of meetings and before the final meeting endorsing a specific action. Japanese businesspeople call this process *nemawashi,* which means "cultivation of the roots."

You also need to learn how to use meetings to achieve your goals. Never go into an important meeting without fully understanding its purposes (both stated and unstated) and having a good idea what other key participants want to achieve from it. Also have clearly in mind what you want to achieve and why you want to do so. Have your key points prepared and memorized and allies identified. During the meeting, listen much more than you talk. Sometimes facilitate discussion by restating other's comments ("Let me see if I fully understand what you just said . . ."), then offer your suggestions and—if a pause presents the opportunity—sum up the overall consensus at the meeting's end. Volunteer to write it down and circulate it to the participants for editing or concurrence and to set up the next meeting. If you can achieve all of this, you have taken some charge of the process and can affect the final outcome. In other words, you have gained some power over the developing situation.

Responsible for Replication

Companies that achieve sustainable success usually have effective succession planning that delivers the right person at the right time to take over the reins. P&G and GE have been superb at developing skillful, well-trained, and experienced leaders ready to take the reins at the right time. It's a sure bet that both of these very successful companies are using the current difficult times to "stretch" and test future leaders with the difficult assignments a recession provides.

As a leader, you have a duty to know when it's time for you to leave and who should replace you. This responsibility has a very long tail. You should continually look for leadership qualities, skills, and traits in the younger people you work with. As you identify these future leaders, you should work to assure that they progress through jobs that will pull them out of their comfort zones, teach them new skills, and give them the experience necessary to replace you and others in your class at the right time. One of the paramount objectives of this process is to test their worthiness to lead (and their ethicality) by assigning them tough tasks. As Abraham Lincoln said, "If you want to test a man's character, give him power." [xxi]

What Toyota and the Best-ever Coach Share

John Wooden—the only person ever elected to the Basketball Hall of Fame as both player and coach—was America's most successful and victorious coach of all time in any sport. During his coaching career at UCLA, he and his teams set records likely never to be matched, let alone broken: 88 consecutive wins, 10 national championships over 12 years—7 of them consecutive, and a career winning percentage of more than 80 percent. Wooden was the classic "pushing" leader. What do this quiet, unassuming former high-school teacher from Indiana and Toyota share? Methodology, including a fanatic focus on detail and continuous repetition. Here's a sample of vintage Wooden thoughts:

- The "luckiest" person is the one who works the hardest. There are no shortcuts . . . no substitutes for the basics. And the first basic is good, old-fashioned hard work. Failing to prepare is preparing to fail.
- If you prepare fully, you may be outscored, but you will never lose. The value created by preparation—the journey—is the reward. Winning is just the destination.
- If you don't make mistakes, you're not reaching far enough.
- When you see a winner, you can be sure you are looking at an individual who pays great attention to perfecting minor details.

And Wooden focused meticulously on seemingly minor details. For example, he began each season by teaching his new players how to put their socks on properly (smoothly with no wrinkles) and tie their shoelaces (firmly with a double knot) in order to minimize the chance of blisters. He didn't allow mustaches or long hair that could gather sweat and flick it into a player's eyes. He demanded courtesy, cleanliness and orderliness; his teams were famous for leaving locker rooms on their own and other college campuses cleaner and neater than they found them.

Not surprisingly, his coaching method was based on what he had discovered about how the human brain learns: (1) Explain (2) Demonstrate (3) Have player imitate (4) Correct (5) Player repeats until the action becomes automatic. As we'll explain later in the book, this "learning" methodology activates a biochemical process in the human brain that underlies all human success—individual, corporate and national. Like all successful coaches and also successful companies like Toyota, Wooden's methods focused on process and used repetition to achieve mastery. [xxii]

Leadership Lessons from the Ledge

So what tools and techniques should we put in the leading drawer? The selection process begins with a personal story. In my teens, I was what swimming instructors called "negatively buoyant," a contradictory term meaning I sank like a stone unless I moved my hands and feet very enthusiastically. When I later joined the Navy, part of officer training was an "abandon-ship" drill requiring a jump into deep water from a ledge about twenty feet above it. This frightened me nearly to death. I later experienced some of the same feeling when asked to lead my first business team.

Like leaps of faith into deep water, leading became easier with experience. I observed senior executives, analyzed, adopted or adapted the best of their techniques, and practiced on my peers until I built a style that was comfortable and relatively effective. Here are the most important leadership lessons I learned.

- Your primary task is to connect and commit your people to each other, to you, and to the best interests of the organization. You can't achieve the authentic communication required to do so without emotion. But depend primarily on facts if you want to persuade people to follow.
- You're only as good as those around you. Hire people smarter than you and <u>listen</u> to them. If you're smart and articulate, this can be hard to do. You may instead tend to unintentionally discourage the challenging debate that can make decisions better. Don't do it. Learn to listen and learn before you talk.
- Don't waste time, effort, and anxiety on things you can't affect.
- Accept responsibility only if you also receive the authority to fulfill it. This can be difficult to do. In Japanese companies, for example, spans of control can sometimes have fuzzy borders that create gray areas. If you encounter a gray area, move in before your neighbor does.
- Check your title and ego at the meeting-room door. Arrogance is counter-productive and ambition belongs in the gas tank, not at the steering wheel.
- Leadership can require theatricality. For example, sometimes as I came through the door into a meeting with subordinates I would throw my expensive suit jacket into a corner, pull my tie down, and roll my sleeves up. The visual message? "See, I have taken off my badges of authority. Let's be honest and outspoken while we are in here working together."
- Although badges of office can make people beside and below you reluctant to be candid, they can be important to those above you. Dress for the job you want, not the one you have. Looking like a leader can help you become one.
- Don't hide in your office sending e-mails. Nothing can beat walking around and talking with people face-to-face. Also

establish a channel you trust where confidential sources can be fully candid about what is happening.
- It's best to have people work *with* you, not *for* you. *For* can create envy and resentment. *With* usually helps to create trust and teamwork.
- Listen carefully and take time to comprehend. "Let me see if I understand what you just said" is a useful way to successfully close a communication loop.
- Someone once said, "Don't let the apparently urgent tyrannize the genuinely important." Find time to *reflect*, one of the most important leadership skills. I used my airplane time.
- Failure belongs to you; victory belongs to your people. Credit and reward them for success and help them learn from failure. Let me emphasize that. Help your people squeeze all the learning they can out of mistakes and use it to improve.
- When sacrifices must be made, give back more than your people and make sure they see you do it. Ethical and effective symbolism again.
- Use brutally honest self-examination to find your blind spots. Then try to work around those you can't eliminate. Many companies put their employees through training to help them develop this skill. If it's available, take it.
- Except in a crisis, coach—don't command. "What do you think?" followed by an intense stare usually yields something much more useful than your own advice and it forces your people to think, learn and develop.
- Assign experienced, senior managers as mentors to promising juniors. This is a primary delivery system for "deep learning" and a pathway for the enlightened succession that can help make companies successful over the long term.
- Polish your people-picking skills so you can match managers with situations where they have a good chance to succeed,

- benefiting both themselves and the company. This skill—at which I was not very good—is vital.
- People will live *up* or *down* to your expectations. Make goals clear and demanding. Then empower, encourage, and support your people to reach. Help those who can't or won't find a job somewhere else.
- When competitors notice them, you will lose some of your best and brightest because your lean structure has insufficient promotion room. Don't create unjustified expectations and resentment by inventing false titles and unnecessary structure to keep them. This expensive, short-term tactic won't satisfy them and it will anger others and weaken the organization. Instead, keep in touch and try to hire them back when you have a proper place for them. I learned this painful lesson by doing it wrong.
- Be open, but not easy. Put your principles on display, but also be willing to respectfully listen to others.
- Never confuse popularity with respect. The first is nice, but the second is vital. And remember that you must give it to get it.
- Always walk your talk; everyone is watching.
- Start every day by asking, "How can I create value?" Finish every day by asking, "What value did I create?"
- Be paranoid. At least once a week, ask yourself and your people: (1) What in our environment has changed? (2) Can it affect our organization? (3) If so, is it a threat or an opportunity? (4) What actions—if any—do we need to take?
- When you inevitably encounter someone who will not follow and even tries to undermine your leadership, convince them to resign or fire them (after constructing the proper paper trail in case they sue).
- Never confuse your ass with the chair it's sitting in. The job is important; you aren't.

- Be biased toward action. Thorough analysis is essential, but you can't allow a faster competitor to put you on the defensive—unless he's wrong; then let him beat you out of the starting gate and—after he's out of sight—take a different path.
- And finally, remember that your final crowning goal is to coach yourself out of leadership, leaving the organization stronger and in better hands than you found it.

I discovered many of these very demanding lessons by <u>not</u> doing them and then trying to learn from my mistake and modify my behavior into more productive pathways. Some of my hard-learned lessons will fit your particular leadership style; some won't.

But the most important lesson I learned is the absolute need for leaders to define, communicate and defend the organization's center (values, vision, strategy and mission all wrapped up in the company culture). If you do so persuasively, people will understand the vital need for it. If you work hard, listen to them, use what they teach you, continually improve, and don't flinch when hard decisions must be made, they will respect you. And if you consistently follow these leadership practices with as much charm, good nature, and fairness as you can, people usually will do what you want them to when you want them to do it.

Controlling

Balancing Cost, Creativity, Discipline and Deviation

Controlling is the most expansive management function. In fact, I'm not sure it deserves its own drawer because so much of it is buried in the other drawers. For example, it's the "C" (for check) in the PDCA cycle that is part of "Planning"; it's the function of Key Performance Indicators (KPIs) in the "Organizing" drawer; it's at the heart of the rating process every time you sit down with a manager to review her performance; and it's the intention of Management By Objectives (MBO). Control wants to invade everywhere, but there are places in the organization it must not be allowed to go. One of those places is the creative process leading to disruptive, break-through products that can seize first-mover competitive advantage.

Innovation is a challenge to control because of the way it evolves and because of the risk inherent in attempting something not done before, such as pushing the development and use of lithium-ion batteries despite the resulting fires in everything from laptops to airliners.

Some experts insist that innovation can be fostered by the right company culture—a kind of corporate petri dish in which genius sprouts. While certain corporate practices may help to optimize the opportunity for its appearance (an ample R&D budget, forming "idea" teams of people with diverse backgrounds, close observation of customers using a current product to discover weaknesses that offer opportunities to improve it or displace it with a new product), I don't believe you can plan and control innovation with the relative certainty you can something like a budget. It's not that predictable.

The birth process for breakthrough products that ignite mass purchasing passion rarely progresses at a measured pace from inspiration to patent to prototype to production to popularity to profit. It jibs and jags, jumps and slumps, darts and dodges, rocketing and ricocheting its way up the curve of creation, often retracing already traveled ground at a different pace with a new perspective. Sometimes, it doesn't make it all the way to the marketplace, instead deflecting into an expensive dead end. This makes it vulnerable to the "control" black belts who might call it waste, kill it, and recycle the resources.

Innovation—particularly in relatively commoditized businesses like the auto or airline industries—also can be over-rated. Time and again, huge, fast-following GM overwhelmed Ford's pioneering introduction of a new product or segment (for example, Mustang), trumping creativity with quick-following similarity and sheer retail mass.

Toyota has adapted its people-centric culture to create a very effective and efficient product development process. Jeffrey Liker, Jim Morgan and Michael Kennedy of the University of Michigan have spent decades studying Toyota's process. Kennedy's book (*Product Development for the Lean Enterprise: Why Toyota's System is Four Times More Productive*) reports that Toyota develops a new car in half the time at half the cost of its competitors. The keys to Toyota's system are (1) entrepreneurial leadership, (2) responsibility-based planning and control, (3) an expert engineering workforce with long and deep experience and (4) concurrent engineering that enables full use of innovation without risking high-quality on-time product launches.

Control is vital in the post-creative processes that commercialize the fruits of creativity; the corporate skills which assure that products are delivered on time, in sufficient quantity, at the lowest possible cost, and at the highest possible quality. These follow-up skills build customer satisfaction and market domination.

Rooting out wasted or underutilized resources and recycling them into more productive uses is probably control's most explicit use. This prospecting/recycling process requires three tools: a ruler, a pencil, and a shovel. The ruler is to measure the gap between results and goals and trigger the PDCA cycle that relentlessly tries to close it. The pencil is to draw borders for people to stay inside of or to breach—under a leader's direction—with new ideas for improving productivity and quality while reducing cost. This continuous improvement of existing products delivers profit for reinvestment in new products. And the shovel is for digging *out* root causes and digging *up* treasure.

Finding the root cause of a problem is like removing a stubborn weed with a long tap root. If you don't dig way down and get all of it, the weed will simply grow back. At Toyota, the heart of the digging process is called "the five whys." When you think you have totally uncovered the root cause, ask yourself why you think so. When you think you have completely answered yourself, you are likely to discover that you need to dig some more. Keep repeating this procedure until you are certain that you have dug all the way down to the tip of the root. Unless circumstances force a premature decision, you should devise and implement a solution only when you have the entire root in your hand.

You also need to dig for the "treasure" (waste) in everything you do, extract value from it that you can use elsewhere, and apply controls to prevent it from cropping up again.

A value chain is simply the collection of activities that provides products or services to customers. It includes (among others): market research, product design and development, component and part production, manufacturing and assembly, sales, service and recycling—in short, virtually every activity included in a modern company. That's one reason why the control function is buried all over the toolbox and is so vital to success.

If every step of the long process from materials to market is not continuously examined and controlled to minimize input while maximizing output, waste will occur. Earlier, I described an optimized "just-in-time" (JIT) value chain where the sourcing of parts from suppliers that begins production is activated only by the "pull" of true customer demand at the other end of the chain.

In the "Organizing" section, I warned of the temptation to activate idle production capacity in reaction to the "push" of expensive structure and the pressure it creates to book a profit. This can stack up unsold inventory (both parts and finished products) in the value chain. In other words, it sucks in and transforms capital, labor, and material into idle, sit-around "just-in-case" waste instead of customer-pleasing, profit-making value.

Remember, productivity is achieved by minimizing the cost of input and maximizing the value of output. Reducing supplies of parts and finished goods at your facility is a mirage if you don't police the entire value chain. Even if you don't see them, parts stored at your suppliers or finished goods stored at your distributor are waste, the price of which will be added to what they charge you or deducted from what they pay you. Waste devours profit wherever it sits along the path from supplier to customer.

But reducing waste by reengineering a sloppy process or implementing just-in-time (JIT) parts delivery is only one of the benefits provided by a lean system. Switching to JIT from JIC (just-in-case) also can reveal other problems lurking within your production process.

Think of it as lowering the level of a river to reveal the rocks disrupting smooth flow so you can dig them out. When a worker can no longer reach for a stored-on-the-premises JIC part to cover a process flaw, the energy-devouring kinks and glitches that create friction and slow or disrupt the river's flow become visible. This enables you to find and dig out the root cause rather than slapping a band-aid on a wave. In this way, avoiding waste also helps to assure quality.

Time and human energy are expensive resources that can easily be wasted by inattentive management. Reworking defective products eats up both. Product development also can gobble up an inordinate amount of time and energy, putting you behind faster competitors who will seize the first-mover advantage you wanted to grab. That's why good managers use <u>concurrent</u> (all areas working simultaneously), not <u>consecutive</u> ("I'm done with my portion, now you can begin yours.") engineering to collapse time, reducing man hours and cost.

Excessive energy usage also can drive costs up. Despite short-term ups and downs, over the long term, the cost of conventional energy will inexorably rise because it is created from ultimately limited resources much in demand by rapidly growing economies such as China and India. Cap-and-trade measures to address global warming favored by the current Washington administration also would incentivize business to further reduce energy usage. Shipping costs would have to be continually reduced. This would require shortening supply lines by, for example, co-locating key suppliers (particularly of bulky or heavy components) around final assembly operations instead of continuing to rely on a geographically dispersed supply chain. This strategy would be further accelerated by companies' efforts to reduce their carbon footprint because obtaining parts from distant sources generates road, rail and air emissions that have a negative environmental impact.

In addition, if you don't closely and continuously monitor your entire supply chain, you put your organization's reputation at risk. A *Business Week* article titled "Made in China, Sued Here"[xxiii] described the increasing number of lawsuits being filed against US corporations with tainted overseas supply chains. Lawyers have gone after companies such as Del Monte, which sold pet treats made with tainted Chinese ingredients.

A Wall Street Journal article by Emily Parker highlights the anything-for-profit attitude behind China's contamination crises.

"Some Chinese will protest that the current wave of panic—which came to a head with restrictions by America's FDA on several kinds of Chinese seafood—is overblown, and the majority of Chinese goods are perfectly safe. But others don't want to live in an environment where brushing your teeth can be a death-defying act."[xxiv]

Ms. Parker sums up the situation this way. "In a country without a real rule of law, where everything is subject to Communist party interpretation, there is no codified set of ethics to guide national behavior."

Another WSJ article by Jeremy Haft highlights how difficult it is to assert control in an era of global sourcing. "On average, it takes China seventeen separate parties to produce a product that would take us three. China's industries are composed of hundreds of thousands of tiny factories and firms—plus traders, brokers, haulers, and agents, all of whom take control of the goods and materials but add little value to the product. With every additional player in the chain, cost, risk, and time grow. In this environment, effective quality control is difficult."[xxv]

The Chinese government reacts in a uniquely direct way to companies that create dangerous or toxic products. They execute the CEO. Although the US government doesn't yet shoot guilty CEOs, the message for American companies is clear. If you source globally to control cost, you must police your entire supply chain or your company's reputation may be tarnished and you may be jailed.

Now let's turn to the type of disciplined management processes that can help you avoid many kinds of trouble: Toyota's method for creating competitive advantage—Hoshin Kanri.

Hoshin Kanri
Putting Your Management Tools to Work

How Toyota develops People, Processes and Organizations
By Bob Bennett

Now that you understand how to use the planning, organizing, leading and controlling tools, let's apply them to your situation. You **Plan** by setting objectives, analyzing problems, and developing plans to achieve the former and resolve the latter. Then you **Organize** people and resources to carry out the plans, **Lead** the implementation, and exercise **Control** by checking results and extracting lessons to incorporate into your next PDCA cycle. We will talk later about Toyota's Lean System Thinking methods to collaboratively engage the talents of managers at every level to dramatically improve both the planning and implementation of top management's strategy, policy and objectives.

These four management functions are drawers in one toolbox for a very important reason. The same tools sometimes show up in more than one drawer, which requires you to understand their interrelationships. Each tool also works better when integrated into a total management system (the toolbox) and a business culture conducive to their effective implementation. Lean System Thinking demands that we create a <u>system</u>, not just a collection of "parts."

Integrating the parts into a whole creates synergy that expands our capabilities, enabling world-class performance. Here are some problems that can occur when isolated activities are individually improved, but <u>not</u> properly integrated.

Functional Improvement	System Sub-optimizing Impact
o Improving labor productivity	Increasing production lot quantities reduces labor downtime by reducing changeovers of machine tooling and production lines. But it takes longer to produce larger lots, lengthening supply lead-time, hurting on-time delivery and requiring larger inventories that drive up related carrying costs.
o Reducing piece costs from suppliers	Quality may suffer, minimum order quantities and lead-times may increase
o Reducing inventories	Safety stocks and buffers that protect customers and internal operations from problems and volume fluctuation are reduced below system's capability (customers suffer and internal chaos caused by expediting destroys process discipline)
o Designing better products	New design requirements exceed current manufacturing capabilities, delaying launch or delivering quality problems to customer.
o Using incentives to temporarily increase sales	Incentives pull future demand forward, creating workload spikes and valleys and related costs with little net impact on long-term revenue. The "lumpy demand" prevents accurate demand forecasting.

Because these impacts are separated by place and time, management often does not recognize the cause-effect relationships. Recognition requires what Toyota calls the "3 Cs"—Consideration, Cooperation and Communication (elements of System Thinking)—to synergistically link the parts of the whole, increasing the leverage of the organization's improvement initiatives.

To help you understand and apply Lean System Thinking, let me share three subjects:

1. System Thinking
2. Strategy Deployment (Hoshin Kanri)
3. How individuals, groups, departments, and organizations develop expertise.

System Thinking

The Fifth Discipline: The Art and Practice of the Learning Organization, by Peter M. Senge[xxvi] describes system thinking, the cornerstone of the five disciplines of a learning organization. It is required reading if you want to understand how two-dimensional linear "cause-effect" perception blinds managers to the three-dimensional realities around them.

Let's use global warming as an example. If I drive a 12-mpg SUV to work today, I will put more carbon emissions into our planet's atmosphere than if I drive my 40-mpg Toyota Avalon Hybrid. But this will not increase the temperature tomorrow, so I do not see the cause-effect relationship. In fact, the temperature change may occur in a different location (separated by distance) and definitely after a delay (separated by time). So it is easy to see why causes of problems in a system can go unrecognized and unresolved.

I first encountered Senge's work in the 1980s. A supplier who was a member of an MIT consortium exploring system thinking invited me to an annual conference where 18 major corporations and MIT faculty presented case studies of applying system thinking to their businesses. They were achieving absolutely transformational changes in thinking, processes and results! I immediately saw how system thinking mirrored Toyota thinking, making it much easier for me to explain Toyota's methods to colleagues and business partners who had not been exposed to Toyota's culture in Japan. I also prepared some training slides to give my managers a deeper understanding of System Thinking. Then together we proved to our customers and competitors how effective Lean System Thinking can be. Between 1993 and 2000, we made my division (responsible for Toyota's North American service parts supply chain from suppliers to dealers and their customers) twice as efficient as its competitors, providing the industry's best service with half the inventory!

Hoshin Kanri: Key to Driving System Thinking Across the Organization

Because Hoshin Kanri overlaps all four drawers of management tools, we have placed it in this overview section on how to implement and manage effective process improvement. Wikipedia calls it "policy **deployment**, **hoshin planning**, or simply **hoshin** (deployed hoshin plan and/or objectives); a strategic planning/management methodology based on a concept popularized in Japan in the late 1950s by Professor Kaoru Ishikawa. Ishikawa understood the power of combining the scientific methods of quality control with the talents of a fully empowered workforce: "Each person is the expert in his or her own job, and Japanese TQC (Total Quality Control) is designed to use the collective thinking power of all employees to make their organization the best in its field." Interestingly, Sakichi and Kiichiro Toyoda were 20 years ahead of Ishikawa in valuing the thinking power of all employees when they committed in 1936 to "create an auto industry in Japan using the brains of Japanese people."

Delegation of authority is the fundamental principle of *hoshin kanri*. In his book, *What Is Total Quality Control?* Professor Ishikawa describes it this way: "Top managers and middle managers must be bold enough to delegate as much authority as possible. That is the way to establish respect for humanity as your management philosophy. It is a management system in which all employees participate, from the top down and from the bottom up, and humanity is fully respected."[xxvii]

This was demonstrated to me at the Senge MIT conference when a presenter pointed at audience members one-by-one, saying "You do this, You do that, You do this . . ." He described this as making your employees into "Human Doings" that do only what they are told. He contrasted this with a management style that enables "Human Beings" to contribute their full potential to meeting the needs of customers and other stakeholders while increasing their own value to the enterprise and society. This style is achieved only when managers realize that their primary role is to develop their people through problem solving. The first style is 80% Direct/20% Coach. The second is 20% Direct/ 80% Coach.

Adaptations of the concept have since been developed by others, among them Dr. Yoji Akao, that use a Shewhart cycle (Plan-Do-Check-Act) to create goals, choose control points (measurable milestones), and link daily control activities to company strategy.[xxviii] Let's begin by broadly contrasting traditional Management By Objectives (MBO)—a "doings" style—with Hoshin Kanri—a "beings" style.

Management By Objectives (MBO)	Hoshin Kanri
What: - Results management - Annual focus on achieving given objectives in each functional area of the organization	What: - Results and means (the methods used to improve business processes that, in turn, improve results) management. - Annual planning completed under the umbrella of a mid-range (3-5 year) plan that has identified the business processes that require increased capability in order to generate the continuously improving results necessary to achieve both annual and long-term objectives.
Characteristics: - Results-oriented - Top-down direction - Directive - Primarily authority-oriented - Each manager independently make plans for achieving objectives, usually beginning close to the start of the new	Characteristics: - Results and process oriented - Top-down direction triggering bottom-up flow of information and means - Participative—all contribute - Primarily responsibility-oriented - Managers realize their processes are part of a system, so they begin months before the new year to coordinate their next-

year with a focus on developing project ideas to achieve the boss' targets. Implementation is hampered by supporting departments' conflicting projects, priorities, and alternatives—also planned in isolation—resulting in wasted effort.	year process improvement projects with managers of other functions whose support is needed. The focus of this "horizontal coordination" is to use the collective expertise of the enterprise to develop consensus and commitment of support.
• Linear: A one-shot image of effort to reach the Goal. (No feedback, no second chance, just start over from scratch each time)	• Circular/spiral image of how to reach a Goal. (Adds feedback loop and chance for improvement; builds on prior learning)
• Focus primarily on Targets	• Considers entire situation (Target and Means)

• <u>Focus on **Control** of:</u>
 	
  - Resources,
  - People, and
  - Results
	• <u>Focus on **enabling** process problem solving</u>:
	  - Checking of Process
	  - Control of Resources
	  - Development of People to get Results

• Seeking Information relating to Outcomes when checking → blaming	• Seeking Information relating to how it happened when checking → learning

Hoshin Kanri Implementation Methods
Vision, Mission and Values

The key to effectively implementing *hoshin kanri* or any other strategy-deployment method is to align every member of your organization and—if possible—those of the primary business partners in your extended enterprise (customers, suppliers, distributors, et al) with a shared vision of the future you are jointly striving to create, with the reasons for pursuing that vision (your mission), and with the values that will guide everyone's thinking and behavior during the pursuit.

Vision: How do you motivate the people of a large organization and its extended enterprise to take responsibility and create meaningful change? With leadership! You must make your vision clear, compelling and aspirational for everyone by emotionally connecting with each of them in ways that will ignite action. Slick, rational power points alone won't move them. Some of the particular methods for forging an emotional link are described in the chapter on "Leading." But, in general, you must create a clear image of the organization's desired future state ("What we will look like when we're done changing"), defining it clearly and succinctly in a way that emotionally connects with and makes them fiercely want it. For the cerebral employees of Toyota Motor Sales-USA, the rational "To be the most respected and successful automobile company" sparked long-term success. Other companies—particularly those in crisis—may require a more overtly emotional banner.

Mission: How do you best focus the organization to work on the right priorities in the right way to most effectively and efficiently achieve the shared vision? By answering the question "Why are we here?" with a vision statement like the one above. Top management and the senior leadership team must provide consistent direction for the organization's intended role in business and society ("What we should do").

Values: Always important, values become vital when leading transformational change. Why? Change causes fear and uncertainty, particularly among formerly confident senior management whose power and prominence are based on achievements and expertise acquired during long, successful careers. These "Knowers" cling to past successes and the methods used to achieve them. Lean System Thinking requires them to once again become "Learners." Lean

System Thinking challenges their traditional, slow, sequential decision-making process carried out by functional silos with faster, simultaneous collaboration that smashes through silo walls to achieve organization-wide linkage—sharpening focus and speeding response.

Abandoning long-held, trusted ways in order to retain status is a psychologically frightening proposition that can generate a variety of behaviors counterproductive to change. Under pressure, people often feel they need to "do whatever it takes to hit their number." Here are a few examples:

- The supervisor who defers maintenance, training, and keeping accurate data so the "saved" man hours can be directed at producing today's numbers regardless of tomorrow's consequences.
- The impatient manager who commands ("Do it this way!") rather than coaches ("What do you think?") because he doesn't want to "waste" time engaging and developing his people's leadership and problem-solving skills.
- The person competing for a bonus or promotion unwilling to collaborate with their counterpart in another department because doing so would require sharing the credit for success.
- Counterproductive behaviors including shooting the messenger, hiding problems, fudging numbers or putting excessive pressure on people to perform.

The right way is a road leading from where the organization is today to where we want it to be in the future. That future is our Vision. The work we do during the journey achieves our Mission. And our Values are guideposts molding our individual and collective behavior—a way of thinking, relating and performing that keeps us on course, accelerating toward our Vision. Jim has described Toyota's values under the "Toyota Way" heading in the Introduction.

My Experience Deploying Hoshin Kanri in Toyota

Let me share how we went about this at my last and largest assignment as group vice president and general manager of Toyota's newly created North American Parts Logistics Division. First, let me set the stage with a little history so you can better understand our starting point, what kind of problems we faced, and how far we had to go.

Toyota began selling cars in the U.S. in 1958—all made in Japan with parts from Toyota's Japanese suppliers. Toyota Motor Sales-USA (TMS-USA) purchased service parts for its U.S. customers directly from its parent company, Toyota Motor Company, Ltd. (TMC) in Japan, who managed all supplier relationships.

TMC managed almost everything for TMS: procurement, determining service level (individual components or subassembly), packaging engineering and pricing, parts catalogs, parts data system master file maintenance, supplier demand forecasting/order release/logistics/on-time delivery, monitoring and assuring supplier quality, and stocking global inventory requirements in their master warehouses in Japan.

For its first 28 years, TMS-USA was responsible for ordering parts from Toyota Motor Corporation parts depots in Japan to replenish the inventory in the 11 regional warehouses that supplied our U. S. dealers. Over time, TMS began purchasing a few maintenance items and minor accessories locally, but this created minimal capability nowhere near the level required to assume responsibility for sourcing over 100,000 unique service parts from over 500 North American suppliers, along with the numerous other functions still supported by TMC in Japan. These functions included service parts engineering, demand forecasting, supplier development and management, mass production coordination, and many others.

In this new arena, TMS was still a toddler compared to its parent company. We lacked the necessary data systems, expertise, facilities and other infrastructure. Over the next three years, we would have to hire and train 60% more people (growing from 650 to 1,600 associates) to fully assume our new responsibilities. And we were not expert with the methods and tools developed over 40 years in Japan that we would need to create robust Lean processes with suppliers and logistics partners.

But then in April 1986, the first Toyota Corolla FX-16 rolled off the line at NUMMI (New United Motor Manufacturing Inc., a joint-venture plant re-opened by GM and Toyota in Fremont, California). With many parts still coming from Japanese suppliers, sheet metal and plastic molded parts made on the premises at NUMMI, a relatively small number of assembly parts sourced from a small number of North American suppliers, and minimal service-parts support for a trickle of new vehicles finding their way onto American roads, the initial tug of increased demand for North American-sourced parts was deceptively gentle—like a small, retreating wave tickling your toes as you stand barefoot on a sunny beach. The challenges, initial learning curve, and small volume of new work were easily coordinated by adding patches to our old legacy data systems. But offshore the tsunami was gathering.

The "NUMMI Miracle"—as U.S. news media christened it—began in 1984 when GM's Roger Smith and Toyota's Eiji Toyoda agreed to re-open a shuttered GM plant in California to build vehicles for both companies. Toyota wanted to see if the Toyota Production System (TPS) could be successfully transplanted onto American soil. GM wanted its top young managers exposed to TPS so that they could transfer its "secrets" into GM's other plants. GM agreed to let Toyota run the plant while Toyota agreed to staff it from the pool of laid-off United Auto Workers and allow the UAW to represent them.

In just two years under Toyota management, what had been GM's worst quality and worst labor relations plant became its best. This experience gave Toyota executives the confidence to fully commit to rapid expansion of North American vehicle assembly and sourcing of production and service parts from local suppliers beginning with a huge, wholly-owned plant in Georgetown, Kentucky.

Less than 6 years after NUMMI's production of the first American-built Toyota, the company had added three more new plants, bringing annual North American production capacity to 1.2 million vehicles. Toyota also was sourcing both assembly and service parts from over 600 North American suppliers, and had exported 400,000 American-made cars to 25 countries in Asia, Europe and the Middle East that also required North American-sourced service parts.

By this time, TMS-USA's annual service parts and accessory sales had rocketed past $2.2 billion and North American suppliers were providing half our needs. But almost all of Toyota's service parts procurement and logistics expertise, data systems, engineering functions and support functions were still in Japan, performed by managers and staff with little or no English skill.

It took two years of coordinated analysis and study to develop a plan. There was a lot of debate about the capability of Americans to take leadership over their geographical piece of the global operation. There were three reasons for the debate.

1. From its beginning in 1957, TMS-USA was staffed with managers recruited from the U.S. domestic auto industry and operated with considerable autonomy from the manufacturing parent in Japan. Presidents of the new North American plants launched from 1984-1991 (NUMMI, TMMK, TMMC, TMMI) were very capable Japanese executives from the parent company. With the help of 200-300 Japanese trainers in each plant, they effectively deployed the Toyota Production System (TPS) and the Toyota business culture in their operations

during the first two years or so after launch. In contrast, we had only four Japan staff in our entire division and they served only as advisors and coordinators, not operating executives.

2. Because our new North American division would have so much functional overlap with vehicle manufacturing, purchasing, inbound logistics, production control, supplier development, and product development engineering, the top-level executives at the parent company directly responsible for the success of our massive project were understandably reluctant to turn over responsibility to an American manager from the sales company.

3. We also were assuming TMC's responsibilities for supplying seven other North American distributors outside the U.S. and driving TMC's global JIT logistics strategy through the entire North American service parts supply chain.

In the end, Eiji Toyoda overruled his Japanese Directors' recommendations and insisted that Americans lead the effort. The new Toyota North American Parts Logistics Division was launched on January 1, 1993, and I was honored to be appointed its first group vice president and general manager and enter the most challenging, exciting and satisfying years of my career. What a tremendous opportunity to learn and positively impact the entire corporation! What pressure to get it right!

The new division became the North American regional headquarters and operations responsible for service parts procurement, warehousing and logistics to supply all eight North American Toyota distributors (United States, Canada, Hawaii, Guam, American Samoa, Saipan, Puerto Rico, and Mexico) plus the global export markets we served. We continued our responsibilities for service parts supply and support to 1,500 U.S. Toyota, Lexus and (later) Scion dealerships. And more than just replicating the traditional batch processes we had, we were challenged to lead a JIT transformation of the entire North

American service parts supply chain from suppliers through our operations to all North American distributors and their dealers. This was the background for the following definition of our mission.

> Toyota North American Parts Logistics Division Mission
> (Comments in italics added for explanation)

1. Provide total parts support to N.A. distributors and global customers

   Globalization added much more comprehensive and complex responsibilities.

2. Develop N.A. suppliers' capabilities to exceed customer expectations

   Because of our lack of Toyota Production experience, we had not yet developed North American supplier capabilities to perform to Toyota's rigorous standards, nor were our capabilities sufficient to provide needed leadership and support to our suppliers.

3. Create industry-leading JIT network from suppliers to customers

   Previously we followed U.S. industry practice, ordering service parts from suppliers monthly and replenishing dealer stocks weekly. We were to lead the industry toward daily JIT ordering and supply from suppliers to dealers.

4. Be TPS/TQM leader for N.A. distributors

   The Toyota Production System and Total Quality Management are internalized in Toyota's DNA in Japan. To successfully lead Toyota's globalization, we had to learn and adapt the Toyota business culture to North America.

5. Partner with associates in mutual growth

> *The Toyota Way will not function without the effective engagement of the full human potential of everyone in the organization; the necessary knowledge to do this effectively is one of Toyota's most significant competitive advantages.*

So, how did we do? We continued to strengthen our industry-leading 98% fill rate to our dealers while reducing replenishment lead-time by 87%. We reduced day's supply of inventory to 50% of industry average—best supply to customers with half the inventory of competitors! We achieved 50% higher labor productivity in our distribution centers and developed the industry's best performing suppliers receiving and supplying orders daily for over 70% of our volume. Our daily inventory replenishment enabled dealers to increase the number of parts numbers they stock by 50% (from an average of 4,000 to 6,000 unique parts numbers for immediate supply to customers) while reducing their inventory investment by 50% and freeing up storage space to convert to service stalls to satisfy more customers and generate more revenue without additional investment.

This was a lot of change for our organization, so we heavily emphasized our values. Achieving management-team consensus on the rock-solid, shared values they will use to guide everyone along the narrow path to success takes a lot more than just printing words on a t-shirt or a plaque in the lobby. Extensive dialogue over a period of time exploring how to eliminate the gap between observed behaviors and the proposed values helps to internalize the deep meaning of each value individually and as a set. The leaders and managers come to serve as constant stewards and examples of the values, "walking the talk" and aligning incentives with the desired behaviors. Consistent values provide the inspiration and assurance that enables employees to change and stretch to create a better future for the enterprise.

What is so hard about this? Apparently a lot. If you read employee posts on GlassDoor.com, you will see that a lot of organizations struggle to live up to their declared values with well-intended efforts to create lasting success, while their finger-pointing management complains about corporate politics, adversarial union relationships and a "younger generation" that doesn't share their work ethic.

Is Toyota perfect? No! But my consulting for other companies has enabled me to understand why Toyota is more effective in living values that more fully engage every employee in customer-focused, aligned and coordinated continuous process improvement and problem solving.

In the early 1920s Sakichi Toyoda founded Toyoda Automatic Loom Works with guiding principles that defined the company's values. The succession of Toyoda family presidents of Toyota Motor Corporation (Sakichi's son Kiichiro who started the automobile division, Kiichiro's uncle Eiji, Kiichiro's sons Shoichiro and Tatsuro, and now Shoichiro's son Akio) have been faithful stewards of Toyota's founding values for over 75 years! I believe the Toyoda family, with only 4% of Toyota stock, has had more positive influence on the company's culture than the Ford family, which at one time owned 40% of the voting stock, has had on Ford Motor Company.

This values consistency has been bolstered by strategic consistency from Toyota's leaders. Though not widely published inside the company, Toyota does have a 50-year plan. The global enterprise always operates under a 5-year mid-range plan. And a strong, conservative "long-term view" is deeply ingrained in the DNA of Toyota's leaders—consistently making decisions that build on the business system processes, relationships and human capital that strengthen organizational capability to achieve long-term goals.

For 76 years the people in Toyota's extended enterprise have lived in a consistent, values-oriented environment with an unwavering line of sight to long-term goals. This has created an incredibly strong alignment that generates tremendous power in the global enterprise. Compare this with other companies that change direction (and often values) with every new CEO or when new economic or business crises arise. Following the latest leadership fad, overextending with acquisitions, retrenching and cutting heads all create a disruptive, reactive environment that forces the organization to keep regrouping and relearning—building up and tearing down—rather than quietly pursuing the continuous plan-do-check-act improvement that gives Toyota its exceptional and growing competitive advantage.

Ponder for a moment the significance of Toyota's consistent values and guiding principles in leading its employees, influencing its business partners and serving its customers and the communities where it does business. Comprehend the cumulative power built up for generations by Toyota's consistent customer focus, values of mutual trust and respect, mutual prosperity, lifetime commitment to develop and utilize the potential of its people, and long-term viewpoint in its dealings with business partners and constituents in communities around the world. So, how can you put all of these same processes into practice? Here's an example.

Simple Example of Rapid Hoshin Kanri Implementation

Several years ago I was supporting the CEO of a $65-million business unit of a global conglomerate. The business had made significant progress in the prior six years under his leadership supported by a lean manager he hired from Toyota. Sales were up 41%, profits up 608%, and customers lost due to past poor delivery were coming back creating the potential for 50% sales growth in the next three years. However, the leadership team lacked the alignment, cross-functional processes and action plans to capitalize on the growth opportunities their production planning and operations improvements had created.

To expedite their progress with limited time and budget, I spent two days interviewing members of the management team and drafted planning documents for the total leadership team to discuss and modify, reaching consensus in order to lead their subordinate managers in developing and implementing successful process improvement plans to achieve the strategic goal of 50% sales growth over three years.

Figure 1 provides an example of Vision/Mission/Values. It provides long-term strategic direction for an organization, defining how the employees can work together to transform the enterprise for a better tomorrow.

Vision, Mission and Values
Figure 1

Vision
☞ *Mid-Range Strategies to Achieve Vision*

1. Company will be the customer's first choice in providing innovative aerospace solutions

    ☞ *Perfect Order*
    ☞ *Rapid response to problems*
    ☞ *Lead-time reduction*

2. Company employees create the foundation of success

    ☞ *Safety, Lean and problem solving to develop our people and processes.*

3. Company will produce exceptional growth and value for our people, customers, suppliers and shareholders through our lean culture

    ☞ *50% sales increase by 2010.*

Mission

1. Provide our customers with safe, reliable high quality aircraft components products.
2. Be the supplier of choice for our customers by supporting their mission and being easy and efficient to do business with.
3. Engage every one of our people in our achievement of competitive advantage for their personal development and the dramatic growth of our business in the competitive global marketplace.

Values

- We put the customer first in all of our decisions.
- Our people are our most valuable asset and only sustainable competitive advantage.
- We are partners in running this business, always treating each other with mutual trust and respect.

    o   We are ethical and honest.
    o   We meet our commitments to ourselves and others.
    o   We value diversity of opinion and culture.
    o   We show our respect by assuring the safety of our operations and protection of our people and the environment.

- We are a continuously learning organization, applying Lean "Rules in Use" to every aspect of our business.
- We promptly surface problems, gather facts and data at the site, and scientifically solve the root cause to prevent reoccurrence.
- We are Lean System Thinkers and our collaborative business partner relationships reflect our values of mutual trust and mutual prosperity and operating with a long-term view.

Mid-Range Plan begins the process of translating the Vision/Mission/Values into action. A mid-range (3-5 year) plan is essential for any organization desiring to sustain and enhance competitive advantage because the time horizons for most truly meaningful changes are more than a year. The first year is required just to do the requisite problem-solving to transform processes and implement innovations that lay the foundation for the big results that are the actual target. Contrast this with organizations that plan just a year at a time, often emphasizing improvements in results metrics that must be achieved by the end of 12 months. Managers competing for bonuses, pay raises and promotions based on "hitting your numbers," see no incentive to work on things that will not produce results until a future period. There is even less incentive to help a colleague in another function to achieve his/her goals. This competition to be the best at achieving one's own short-term goals usually generates a lot of sub-optimization.

Additionally, transformational change requires new thinking, risk taking, and confidence that top management will not change direction in the face of competitive actions, economic pressures or the latest fad. The larger and more geographically-dispersed the organization and its business partners, the longer it takes to break the current inertia, align everyone in the new direction, communicate the mid-term strategies, organize teams to develop the plans, and start moving forward—frequently more than a year.

Developing a mid-range plan requires a clear understanding—with facts and data—of the strategic environment and the position of the organization in the environment relative to customers, competitors, suppliers, business partners, and the community. Typically top management and a small group headed by a capable key leader can do this quite efficiently. But I have found that small and mid-size companies often see this as far more complex than it really is. Even large organizations can speed the process by simplifying it.

Figure 2 is an example of the actual mid-range plan developed and adopted by the management team of a $65-million business in less than three weeks. A brief background summarizes the past direction and provides a rationale and target for the next three years (the numbers are disguised). Then following the popular Balanced Scorecard concept, the plan defines and quantifies the current condition, the challenges to be overcome, countermeasures to be developed and 3-year targets in the categories of customers, operations, investments in people and capability, and financial goals.

2008-2010 Mid-Range Plan

Figure 2a

Background

- 2002-2007 Company dramatically improved competitive position:
  - Sales up 41%; profits up 608%
  - On-time delivery improved from 24% to 84%
  - Poised to take business from competitors.
- 2010 Sales potential is $90 million—50% increase from 2008
  - Achieved by increased business with existing customers
  - Requires dramatic improvement in customer satisfaction
- Overarching Goal: Total customer focus to grow 50% by 2010.
  - Every employee has a customer and the talents to satisfy them.

	Current Condition (2007)	Challenges to Growth	Countermeasures	2010 Targets

Customer	• On-time 84%
	• Customer Defect Rate 0.7%
	• Urgent order lead-time 12 days
	• Customer Survey Rating 80%
		• Mature market
		• Few new programs
		• Must win business away from competitors
		• Higher capital investment required for new programs
		• Order intake and management mistakes & L/T
		• Need to listen and respond better
		• AOG & returns management
			• Define customer values to guide desired behaviors
			• Develop Company strategy for up-front investment in new programs
			• Order intake and management process development (timely and accurate; process to manage "created demand")
			• Customer Connection Pilot establishing "rules" & process
				• 97% Perfect Order Index:
				  o On time
				  o Complete
				  o Defect free
				  o Correct invoice
				• Urgent order lead-time 3 days (-75%)
				• Customer Survey rating 95% (+19%)

2008-2010 Mid-Range Plan (Continued)

Figure 2b

	Current Condition (2007)	Challenges to Growth	Countermeasures	2010 Targets

Operational	• On-time to mfg plan 27%
	• Cycle time days 35
	• Cost of quality 4.2%
	  ○ Scrap 2.0%
	  ○ Rework 2.2%
	• Supplier on-time 44%
	• Inventory supply days 80
	• Sales per person $155K
	
	• Late and costly new product launches
	
	• New business: kitting & spares
		• Lack data integrity to accurately plan and manage production schedule
		• Lack tooling quality/setup accuracy to produce planned yield
		• Lack of process standardization → excessive variation and errors
		
		• Lack of standardized processes and poor connections between processes
		• Unique processes required
			• Define operational values
			• Cross-functional project to:
			  ○ Create accurate MRP data and standards
			  ○ Ensure tooling capability and setup accuracy.
			  ○ Implement disciplines to produce the right product at the right time
			  ○ Develop rapid problem solving capability and processes to respond to problems
			  ○ Supplier mgmt program
			• Implement Standardized Work and Practical Problem Solving
			• Develop standardized new product development and launch process
			  ○ Manage cost & schedule milestones
			• Develop kitting & spares processes
				• On-time to mfg plan(+250%) 95%
				• Cycle time days 10 (-71%)
				• Cost of quality 0.5% (-88%)
				• Supplier on-time (+116%) 95%
				• Inventory supply (-233%) 24 days
				• Sales/employee (+29%) $200K
				
				• 80% improvement
				
				• Achieve scheduled plan

2008-2010 Mid-Range Plan (Continued)

Figure 2c

	Current Condition (2007)	Challenges to Growth	Countermeasures	2010 Targets

People	• OSHA recordable rate 3.8 (accidents/200,000 work hours)
	• Development Engineering strength is major differentiator
	  ○ However, we are not effective at preventing and rapidly solving technical problems in production
	• Workforce not engaged in Continuous Improvement
	• Deficiencies in some skill areas
	• New business: kitting & spares
		• Lack of standardization and emphasis
		• Experienced engineers nearing retirement; limited pipeline of talent & no preparation for growth
		• Skill deficiencies include problem solving, critical production skills (welding/ cross-training) and process standardization and discipline
		• New skills/organization required
			• Include safety as first priority in Standardized Work
			• Define people values
			• Human Resources Development, Organization & Succession Plan
			  ○ On-the-job problem solving is primary development method (with necessary training and coaching)
			  ○ Total cross-training program (plan, visual management, recognition & rewards)
			• Identify requirements, prepare and implement plan
				• OSHA recordable rate 0.9 (-75%)
				• 90% of identified critical positions filled with fully competent employee
				• 5 implemented suggestions per employee per year
				• Achieve annual targets for training → on-the-job implementation
				• Achieve plan commitments

Figure 2d

2008-2010 Mid-Range Plan (Continued)

	Current Condition (2007)	Challenges to Growth	Countermeasures	2010 Targets
Financial	• Sales $65.2 million • Material cost of sales 31.1% • Direct Labor cost of sales 24.9% • VOH percent of sales 7.6% • FOH percent of sales 19.0% • G&A and Sales OH 6.9% • Operating Profit $6.7 million (10.4% of sales vs. 15% target) • Cash flow $4.6 million	• Cost competitiveness • Growing low cost country competition • Rising material and people costs • Metrics alignment with Lean • Standards do not meet profitability needs. • Make vs. Buy strategy is unclear	• Establish financial metrics for every value stream and functional area • Use Lean to engage organization in the total elimination of waste • Review and revise metrics to encourage Lean Thinking • Support Operational MRP data accuracy project • Management develop criteria, then team develops and tests strategy through pilot projects	• Sales $90 million • Material % of sales 30.6% • Direct Labor % of sales 19.9% • VOH % of sales 7.0% • FOH % of sales 18.0% • G&A and Sales OH 6.9% • Operating Profit $15.3 million (17% of sales) • Double cash flow as a percent of sales $12 million • Complete make vs. buy strategy by Aug. 2008

A comprehensive, clear and easy to visualize mid-range plan provides the overall framework to guide top management in development of each year's plan.

It also provides direction for managers' annual planning of the process improvement actions needed to achieve the 3-year plan.

Company Annual Policy and Objectives prioritize the "how" (top management policy direction on approach or purpose to achieve our objectives) and the "what" (the specific quantitative objectives to be used to measure success for the year). This will direct efforts of the organization's managers to develop their individual and coordinated action plans to improve the organization's processes to the higher level needed to achieve the year's objectives.

A lot of coordinated effort is needed to be fully aligned and ready to go to work at the beginning of the new year, so top management should initiate the necessary annual planning process as early as five months before the end of the current year. Far too often we see companies not finalizing their annual objectives and action plans until the third or fourth month of the new year, forcing managers to accelerate actions (without full knowledge of their process problems), cut corners, "slash and burn," and sub-optimize to hit their functional silo objectives. Requiring the organization to cram 12 months of process improvement efforts into 7 or 8 months is a failure by senior management.

The following schedule provides an example of when to start and how much time to allow your organization to plan effectively and be "ready to hit the ground running" from the start of the new year. ("N" is the first month of the new year):

N-5:

- The Mid-Year Annual Plan Review meeting completed the previous month will provide a comprehensive understanding of progress on process improvement project work and business

results for the first six months of the years. Additionally, adjustments to Annual Plan action plans will by now be thoroughly deployed to achieve current year objectives.
- Planning staff and company managers can begin the process of reviewing YTD results (e.g., sales, operations, improvement projects, financial) and estimating year-end results and remaining problems.
- External analysis, including changes to customer needs, market trends, competitive actions and plans, economic forecast, regulatory changes, new technologies, etc.
- Internal analysis, including SWOT, capabilities (advantages and disadvantages), new technologies/products, etc. This should include a review of the Mid-Range Plan, the progress towards its Vision and Goals, and areas needing attention in the plans for the coming year.
- Benchmarking areas targeted for improvement, being certain that you understand the processes your benchmark used to achieve best-in-class results

N-4:

- The assessment process picks up as priorities, key issues, and new opportunities start to emerge. Key management and the planning staff begin to consider how the coming year will be different and what the company might do to respond. For most companies, the last few months of the year are a busy time, so management must ensure that the PDCA assessment and learning from the current year is being done.
- We want managers to have adequate time to consider the gaps between current business system/business process capabilities (producing today's results) and the capabilities they will need to add (by problem solving to make their processes, people and the manager's personal management capable of higher

level performance). Therefore, discussions about possible KPI priorities and objectives should start now, including consideration of progress against Mid-Range Plan goals. This is the beginning of a "catchball" process vertically and horizontally in the organization to build consensus around what goals to pursue and the abilities and challenges within the organization to improve its process capabilities to deliver to these goals. Leaders of effective Lean organizations encourage and support this dialog and focus attention on understanding the work in their processes to understand what problems should be prioritized for solution.

- While the final objectives for the next year will not be officially announced until early January, at least a general directional understanding of both "Policy" (top management's direction on "how" the annual objectives should be achieved) and the "Objectives" (the KPIs top management defines to quantify the targets for the organization to achieve) is needed.

NOTE: Quantitative KPIs make targets and gaps from current performance crystal clear. This clarity enables responsible managers to determine which business processes to improve in order to close the gaps and targets to better understand the problem solving actions and cross-functional support needed to be successful.

N-3:

2008 Annual Policy and Objectives — Figure 3

Policy—How to Achieve Objectives	Objectives—Metrics to Measure Progress	
Customer—Grow business with best customer service and rapid response to problems	1. Perfect order index 2. Order-to-delivery lead-time days 3. Urgent order lead-time days 4. Customer survey results (+12.5%)	92% 20 7 90%
Operational—Total customer focus by every employee to improve business processes	5. On-time to production plan 6. Cycle time days (-50%) 7. Cost of quality % of sales (-70%) 8. Supplier on-time (+100%) 9. Inventory days supply (-50%) 10. Sales per employee (+15%) 11. New product launch efficiency	95% 17 1.4% 88% 40 $178,000 +60%
People—Develop full human capacity of all our people by applying new learning to solving problems on the job	12. OSHA recordable accidents (-50%) 13. 8 hours training per employee 14. Problem solving projects completed 15. Kaizen implementation reports 16. Jobs cross trained 17. HR development & succession plan	1.9 3,200 100 400 500 8/'08
Financial—Increase the productivity of our equipment, materials, space and people to improve price competitiveness	18. Sales 19. Operating profit (15% of sales) 20. Cash Flow (+74%)	$68 MM $10.2 MM $8 MM

- Not later than the beginning of month N-3 (i.e., October for companies who plan on a calendar year basis), all-manager meetings should be conducted to review the planning process and expectations and provide necessary guidance for managers to start their planning activity. This may include:

    o Review Vision/Mission/Values, mid-range plan and progress
    o Review New Year Planning Environment document and proposed New Year Annual Policy & Objectives

o   Direction to each manager to complete a "Year-End Review" of their actions to achieve the current year's Annual Plan objectives, with an emphasis of documenting the lessons learned and the remaining problems to be solved to provide input to their next year's Annual Plan. A non-blaming, humble self-reflection (*hansei*[2])—"How can I do better next time" attitude is necessary for learning and improvement. After drafting the Year-End Review, start developing an Annual Plan of process improvement action plans to solve remaining problems and achieve the anticipated policy and objectives for the coming year.

Figure 4 illustrates the Annual Plan planning and management cycle (PDCA):

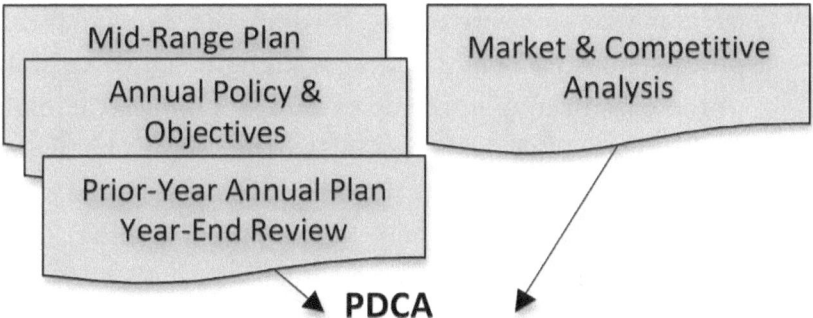

Hoshin Kanri Annual Plan PDCA Cycle Figure 4

PLAN: Each Manager prepares an Annual Plan of priority business process improvement projects:

Dept/Manager_____			**Annual Plan**				Date_____						
#	Objective	Target	Resp	J	F	M	A	M	J	J	A	S	O	N	D	Sptg Dept

DO: Excellent discipline and cooperation in process improvement problem solving, managed at every level of organization.

CHECK: Mid-Year and Year End Annual Plan Review Meeting – formal presentation to senior management:

Dept/Manager____		**Year-End Review**				Date____
#	Goal	Target	Key Actions	Eval	Reason	Future Action

ACT: Standardize, sustain, and spread good ideas across organization. Repeat **PDCA**

N-3 ~ N-1:

- Managers work with their subordinates to complete the manager's Year-End Review of their progress against the current year's objectives and to draft the Annual Plan of process improvement actions to strengthen the capability of the organization's business system to produce the higher performance needed to achieve the company Annual Objectives (the "What") in a manner consistent with the Annual Policy (the "How"). Figure 5 contains the Annual Plan format we used with an example:

Figure 5

Annual Plan — Date April 3, 2007

Dept/Manager: Production Control

No	Objective	Target	Resp	Timeline (Jan–Dec)	Sptg Depts
	Jointly with Marketing, reduce demand variation to reduce finished goods inventory	50% demand fluctuation & F/G reduction; PK>97%	JR/JA	Plan & approve pilot (Feb–Mar); Daily order trial (Apr–May); Implement order types/priorities (Mar–Jun); Created Demand leveling trial (Jun–Aug); Develop Supply, Stocking & Production policies with pilot customers (May–Sep); Develop Rollout Plan (Aug–Oct); Rollout to other customers (Oct–Dec)	Mktg Sales Inv. Cont.
	Introduce *heijunka* (level loading) into production scheduling for plant and suppliers	Reduce daily workload hours fluctuation 25%	JA	Standardize/stabilize production scheduling system (Jan–May); Level incoming orders over week (Apr–Jul); Develop Plan for Every Part (PFEP) (May–Jul); Develop Model Heijunka scheduling (Jul–Sep); Implement PFEP in CASA (Aug–Oct); Implement PFEP with suppliers (Sep–Dec)	Lean consultant Purchasing Ft. Wayne Production
	Supplier Connection Improve: Get a clear and binary connection with VSP (shafts supplier)	PPM 3000→300; R/M inv. $850k→$500k; SPAN 15→5 day	JR/JA	Standardize/stabilize VSP project (Jan–Apr); Plan Phase 1 supplier connection program & supplier expectations (Apr–Jun); PFEP (Jun–Jul); Implement PFEP (VSP) (Jul–Aug); Document learning in supplier training PPT (May–Sep); All key supplier meeting (Sep); Begin daily feedback & problem solving (Oct–Dec)	Lean consultant Purchasing Production Plant Mgr

105

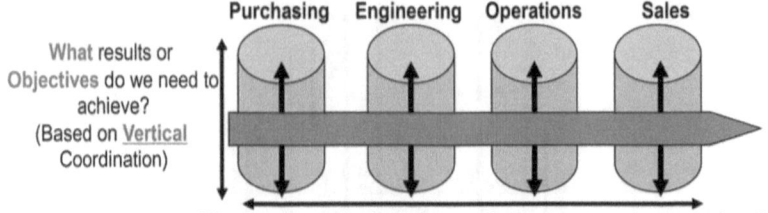

Hoshin Kanri: Purpose x **PROCESS** x People Figure 6
Lean System Thinking requires "Horizontal" communication & cooperation

- Value flows horizontally, so to achieve our PURPOSE we must understand the work to be done in each major PROCESS and the connections between processes.

- Emphasis is on **horizontal coordination** to understand how the entire process works together, and the nature of the work to be done in each process.
  > Observation and data to understand system and functional problem causes.
  > Cross-organizational collaboration for single best solutions and agreed plan.
  > Clear, binary plan and connections between processes and with management.

Source: Mike Hoseus, Center for Quality People & Organizations

- Figure 6 shows the difference between a traditional silo-focused organization's planning (primarily relying on "vertical" coordination to negotiate the objective numbers) and Lean organization planning (primarily relying on collaborative "horizontal" coordination to determine and agree on the process-improvement, problem-solving activities and schedule, using "catch ball" dialogue regarding capability and support.) Then the important collaborating with other managers—especially those who must support one another—begins. Extensive and repeated coordination with supplier and customer processes also must be completed to assure clear agreement on what actions, by whom, by when—accompanied by a "signed-in-blood" commitment. The "rules" for connection between processes also must be defined and agreed upon because no one can achieve and sustain world-class performance if surprised by unanticipated changes to inputs or outputs. Input and consensus must be obtained from stakeholders and upper management. This takes many meetings—often one-on-one—to resolve conflicting priorities, schedules, and proposed solutions and then to revise, review and finally approve plans. These commitments are essential in a business culture where the expectation is that a promised plan will be completed to deliver the promised result. A plan lacking these commitments is an empty promise that "has no meaning." THAT'S WHY THREE MONTHS ARE REQUIRED. But when you are done, everyone is aligned and the focus is on getting it done. This works much better than each manager developing his own plan independently and then spending most of the year competing with other's solutions for the same problem, negotiating for support (too often unsuccessfully), and ending up working independently rather than fixing the broken connections in the process that hinder progress.

In my experience, the key points for management to remember when preparing an Annual Plan are:

- Creating an effective and robust policy deployment PDCA process for managers at every level is by far the most important initial goal. Therefore, use the first year to model the full PDCA process, avoiding the desire to include many process-improvement projects in each manager's plan. Including too many projects will administratively overwhelm the managers, require too much time for reporting, dilute organizational resources, and exceed upper management's capability to provide the necessary attention, coaching and support to develop and implement all of the improvements.

- Limit the Annual Plan projects to problem solving that will substantially improve the capability of business processes, not for routine daily work improvement.
- Begin with a small number of projects. My Toyota division had 47 managers at headquarters and a number of large facilities around the country, yet we found 3-5 projects reported on one A3-size page (11" x 17") challenging enough. We allowed two pages for mid-year and year-end reviews to be certain we did enough PDCA to capture the learning necessary to improve our planning, process-improvement, and problem-solving capability.
- Sustain and improve core management practices by helping managers learn the discipline of time management in order to make upper-management involvement time-efficient. For example, we limited each manager to 10 minutes for reporting and 5 minutes for Q. and A. Managers should report only on projects where they encountered problems that prevented goal achievement (this enables other's support); successful projects should be limited to very brief summaries, if reported at all (You don't need support here). Focus on "What can we do better next time?"
- Assure that the managers' objectives are aligned with company objectives in the Annual Policy & Objectives plan.
- Always document the target with a number that can be tested—like a scientific experiment.
- Break the action plan down into discrete elements that can be managed, measured, and tracked individually.
- Obtain "signed-in-blood" commitments from each supporting department's manager; without them, your plan <u>has no meaning</u>, because you cannot guarantee success to your boss.

N-1: All-manager Year-end Review to summarize accomplishments vs. current year Annual Plan objectives and describe remaining problems to be tackled in the coming year. Only objectives behind target/schedule are reported, as the emphasis is on organizational learning from solving problems and focusing management support where it is most needed. Overall company performance also is reviewed.

N: New Year Kickoff Meeting where company Annual Policy & Objectives and each manager's Annual Plan is presented for senior management review and approval. After the months of work that proceeds this meeting makes the meeting somewhat ceremonial, but it serves very important purposes, including:

1. The participation of senior management from each functional area is very important to assure understanding of and commitment to the necessary cross-functional support of the approved plans.
2. Many commitments have been made to work together as a unified management team to achieve the goals and plans presented at this meeting. Like soldiers marching into battle, we will make every effort, every sacrifice to support and protect our comrades and achieve our mission. The public statement of these commitments makes them even more important to fulfill.

- Each manager's Annual Plan and Objectives are achieved by his people, and little is more important than maintaining their focus on the policies and objectives that top management has deployed as the most important priorities for the business and the manager (with the support of his people) has translated into an action plan and objectives are his top priorities for the year. Making all this all visible is of great value in getting it all done and achieving one's objectives. Toyota has developed what is called a Floor (Worksite) Management System (Figure 7). In fact, "making hoshin visible" all the way down the organization to where the work is done is Toyota's way of "making hoshin usable." Toyota's Floor (Worksite) Management System (Figure 7) does that. To be useful, our plans and objectives (our "hoshin") must be visible to the people who will support implementation. The manager's Annual Plan and progress tracking, as well as visual display of KPIs for results and for process performance, the best practice "rules" we have agreed to follow, the problems we surface when we cannot follow our rules or achieve our planned results, and our problem solving activities can all be displayed visibly where we work to enable workers and managers to engage in the PDCA that enables world-class performance.

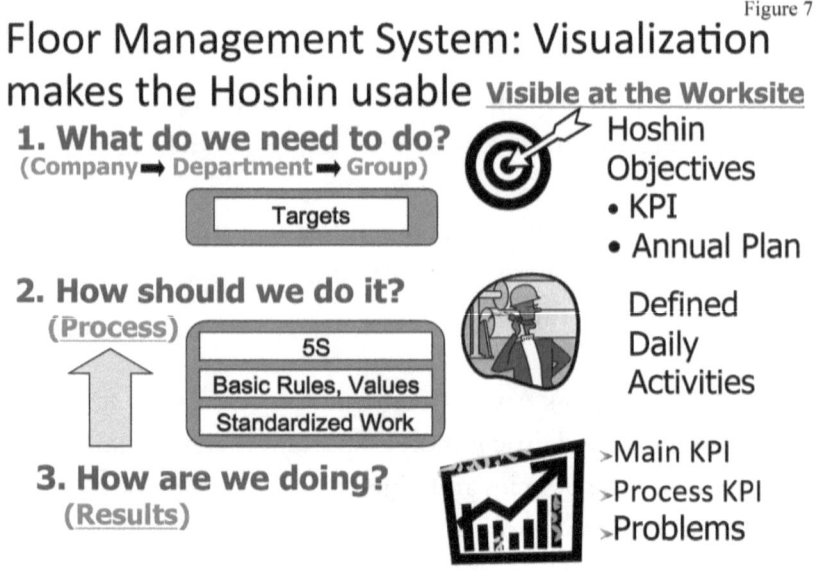

Figure 7

Source: Mike Hoseus, Center for Quality People & Organizations

Mid-Year Annual Plan Review to report progress against the committed plan. As a learning organization, we learn from solving problems, so rather than report his successes, each manager reports on the projects that are behind schedule or tracking below the target. Recognizing that the entire attendance wants you to succeed and is available to support as needed if they understand the problems, causes and future actions you as the responsible manager have found and planned. This *hansei* following the PDCA scientific method enables the management coaching and organizational support for the manager's success and learning enables the company to achieve its objectives while building superior planning and plan management skills in its people.

Although it requires more effort, you may want to start with quarterly reviews to more quickly discover and resolve misunderstandings and problems in this new process in order to recover progress for managers who do not initially grasp what to do.

N+12: Year-End Annual Plan Review: another sharply-focused progress review and report of recovery plans with a continuing emphasis on problem-solving, organizational and management support.

Hoshin Kanri Conclusions

- Managers in every organization—including Toyota—manage results. However, far too many managers wait for the end-of-month reports to learn the results, showing only symptoms of problems.
- Toyota emphasizes developing processes that can be managed "in the moment" to see and understand cause and effect as a problem is occurring and respond immediately to minimize the impacts, recover stability and flow, and capture cause facts and data to quickly begin tackling the root cause. This is one level of PDCA—continuous improvement in daily, weekly and monthly work.

- Hoshin Kanri: Management of the "means" of continuous process capability improvement to achieve targeted results is another level of PDCA—continuous improvement in the annual and mid-range transformational improvement of business and organizational processes and human capability to achieve breakthrough competitive advantage. Remember, the emphasis is horizontal cross-organizational cooperation to improve total business system processes for the benefit of customers and the survival of the enterprise. This collaborative management of the hoshin process takes time and requires structure and discipline. The rewards are value streams that work effectively in unison, gaining traction and producing bigger results faster with far less useless wheel spinning.
- This Lean approach, well developed by Toyota, is dramatically different and a source of competitive advantage for the company over other organizations!

How Toyota Develops Individual, Working Group, Functional, And Organizational Expertise

Controlling takes different forms in different business cultures. In Management By Objectives (MBO) organizations, control is more top down, directive, command-and-control. In Lean System Thinking organizations like Toyota, "distributed leadership" places more focus on developing and enabling people to use their full human potential to effectively contribute to the success of the total organization. This is done through constant problem-solving, which builds a continuous-improvement culture. There is much more focus on melding the "parts" into synergy for the betterment of the whole.

Growing numbers of practitioners and academics are mastering the "tools" of the Toyota Way—standardized work, kanbans, visual control, kaizen, value stream mapping, TPM, A3s, 3P, 5S, etc.—the "artifacts" of Lean one can see. But a much smaller number have grasped the characteristics and elements one cannot see—the business culture and the way it engages people in a very different way. I have been told of research that found that only 19% of CEOs are satisfied with the results of their Lean initiative, as their results are far from Toyota-like. So what's missing?

Because a business culture must be experienced before it becomes truly understandable, it is challenging to explain how Toyota so effectively develops its people and processes to perform so well for customers and the business. So I was pleased when my co-author shared Daniel Coyle's research into how human exceptionalism is developed. For me, the parallels with the Toyota organization's business culture and the contrasts with MBO-type organizations are profound.

Not surprisingly, the Toyota Way takes full advantage of how the human brain learns. In his fascinating and best-selling 2009 book *The Talent Code: Greatness Isn't Born. It's Grown.* Coyle describes human learning as a chemical process—the deposition of myelin caused by repetitive action. Like a computer, the hardwiring of the human central nervous system is composed of electrical circuits (neurons), which scientists call "gray matter." Electric impulses fired down neurons trigger synapses causing action—everything from kicking a ball to swinging a golf club, playing a piano, completing a chess move or making a business decision.

At birth, a neuron is like a bare copper wire that carries the electrical impulses that make our brains function. An impulse leaks, causing the signal to lose focus and slow as it travels down a bare neuron. But each time one is fired, cells called oligodendrocytes reach out and wrap the neuron in a layer of insulating myelin, which scientists call "white matter." Layer by layer, this insulating process reduces leakage, enabling the impulse to retain focus and travel faster—eventually increasing its speed from about 3 to more than 200 miles per hour. These far faster impulses shorten reaction time and sharpen coordination among synapses, which—in turn—improves the skill.

The insulation process is enhanced during "deep practice" at the margin of competence where mistakes are repeatedly committed and corrected, slowly improving the skill as the student climbs to the next level. This biochemical process is the prototype copied by highly successful "learning" companies to sharpen and gather individual skills into coordinated corporate capabilities competitors find difficult to copy.[xxix]

The Talent Code helps us understand how deep practice at the margin of competence grows efficient and effective neural pathways in the human brain. But you also can apply these concepts to your organization and the creation of operational excellence. Just as a person's brain connects to and controls all parts of his body, an organization has an aggregate brain (the individual brains of each person plus the corporate structure, culture, values and communication and operational pathways linking them) that—especially in today's complex global environment—must be extremely fast, accurate and adaptive in synchronizing the functions of its parts. Coyle's work provides profound insight into the way Lean System Thinking helps create the necessary individual and corporate skill, speed and coordination for world-class performance. (The co-author of 'In Search of Excellence', Tom Peter is quoted on the cover of Coyle's book as saying "I am willing to guarantee that you will not read a more important and useful book in this or any other year".)

Before getting into the explanation, let me translate Coyle's terminology into terms that relate to a business organization:

- "Deep practice." Performing a task or activity with full awareness of the ideal performance standards while sensing and comparing the actual performance and understanding the gaps and causes of the gaps to be corrected during the next practice—i.e., performance of the task. (Toyota's culture of stopping work when a problem occurs, makes a problem very visible, providing an immediate—and often

pre-planned—response to the problem, and a "do it now!" philosophy of rapid experimentation to test a better way are methods that support deep practice learning.)
- "Master Coaching." Coyle tells us that talent is a function of "deep practice," "ignition" and "master coaching." You will find in all of my descriptions that follow how leaders at every level of a successful Lean System Thinking organization serve as master coaches in developing the talents of their people.
- "At the margin of competence[1]." Action or performance at the best current level of capability.

    o   The Toyota business culture forces all work to be done at the limit (the "margin") of the organization's current best level of "competence" where "mistakes are repeatedly committed and corrected to create faster, more efficient and better synchronized neural pathways." The business culture includes methods such as the following to constantly identify gaps between performance at the clearly defined "margin of competence" and "mistakes" that cause performance below this level:

    — Clear binary standards and rules are strictly enforced and followed.
    — Excellent performance is expected and quantified so it can be measured.
    — Every process is designed so that "ahead/behind" and "normal/abnormal" are "visible at a glance."
    — Project action plans are broken into small measurable steps, and clear objectives are defined for each review meeting.

- "Mistakes." The gaps between the current level of process discipline or results and the standard defined for the margin of competence. We usually define this through observation of work and set the standard at the level that is "consistently repeatable." For example, if we do 10 time studies of a job, we throw out the one or two exceptionally fast times and select the fastest time that has been repeated three or more times.

- "Repeatedly committed." Expecting consistent high performance at the current best level of capability, each process is highly defined and quantified. Thus even small variations are exposed as "mistakes" to be corrected.
- "Corrected." Repeated mistakes enable repetition of deep practice problem-solving to stabilize and then continuously improve processes and organizational problem-solving skills.
- "Neurons" or "Neural pathways." In addition to Coyle's definition as the gray matter in the brain, I use "neural pathways" as an analogy for the connections along the formal and informal organizational circuits or pathways for communication and interaction between individuals within an organization.
- "Myelin." Insulation deposited in layers upon neurons/neural pathways with each successful deep practice. This insulation greatly increases the speed of an electrical signal and also controls the speed to precisely synchronize multiple signals that must arrive at the same point at the right time (such as controlling the multiple muscles used in hitting a golf ball 200 yards down the center of the fairway). In the organizational analogy, deep practice problem-solving similarly strengthens and protects the neural pathways of your organization. Here, the "myelin" (strengthening of capability) comes from the deep practice required to complete detailed investigations of the work including rooting out causes with collaborative problem-solving, conducting small, quick experiments to test hypotheses before committing to bigger solutions, negotiating among competing priorities and

limited resources, and developing and coordinating detailed action plans with clear deliverables, responsibilities, due dates and targets. All of this also improves the speed and coordination of communications pathways and the human relationships needed for better execution and faster response when problems arise or circumstances change.

How Toyota facilitates effective and synergistic work—Background for explaining how Coyle's work relates to Toyota Business Culture and Exceptional Organizational Performance

- While individuals receive performance appraisals that influence career progression, pay raises and bonuses, Toyota places more emphasis on group and total organization performance, encouraging teamwork, collaboration and cross-organizational cooperation.
- Much greater effort using the scientific method goes into planning and building consensus before starting a project, improving a process or implementing a solution to a problem. Working in teams provides a variety of perspectives and checks and balances—creating many cycles of deep practice that develop group capability. On-site observation of the problem at the point of cause (*genchi genbutsu*: go and see at the *gemba*: the "real place" where the work is done) facilitates full understanding of the problem, its impact and causes, which enables the observers to summarize facts and data so colleagues, stakeholders, supporting functions and management can contribute ideas to improve the solution and commit support. Don't try to solve problems in a meeting room!

- One of a Toyota manager's most important responsibilities is to develop his people's problem-solving capabilities with daily deep practice at the margin of competence, the primary method for human and organizational development. Problem solving is often presented visually on an A3-size (11" x 17") paper with a flow of logic following the scientific method. The result is then presented publicly like a scientific hypotheses tested in an experiment for scrutiny, challenge, input and consensus from colleagues, stakeholders and management. This process—completed before the implementation of solutions—greatly strengthens both individual and group neural pathways, increasing the likelihood of successful implementation.

Examples of Developing Brains and Neural Pathways in People and Organizations—In the Individual, the Work Group, and the Total Organization

1. <u>Individual Person: Daily Work Continuous Improvement PDCA</u>

Brain Cells

O———O

Connected by Neural Pathway

<u>Traditional organizations inhibit identification of individuals' mistakes (i.e., Coyle's gaps "at the margin of competence" between targeted and actual performance) thus limiting the repetitive correction that grows myelin to make neural pathways faster, stronger and better synchronized</u>. Examples:

- A focus primarily on steps in the process rather than strictly applied standards for how the steps of the job should be done and the expected outcomes.

- A focus on results, while ignoring the process used to achieve them (too often working around problems in the defined process and/or sub-optimizing the system).
- Discouraging the exposure of problems ("shoot the messenger").
- Encouraging subordinates to bring problems to managers for solution rather than solving them without assistance ("80% direct/20% coach")

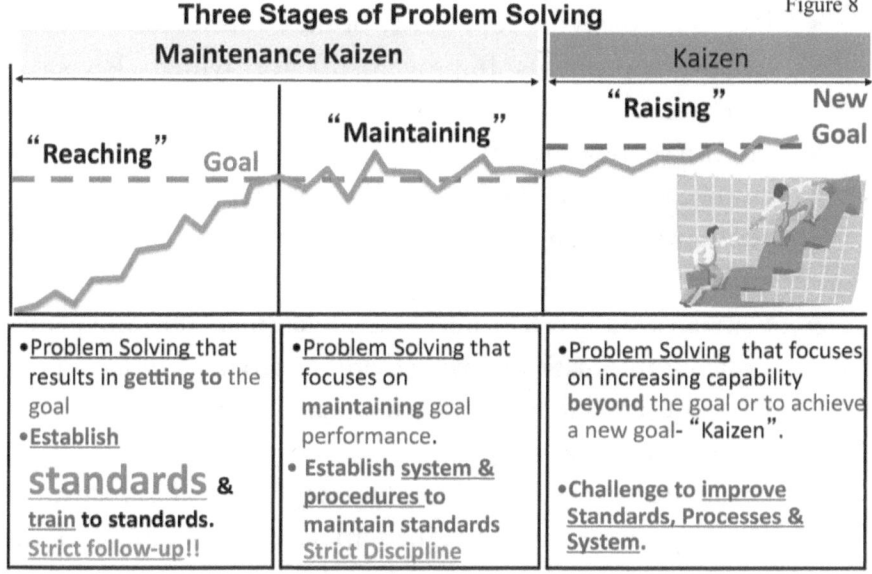

Figure 8

Source: Mike Hoseus, Center for Quality People & Organizations

<u>In contrast, Toyota facilitates each individual employee's deep practice to grow ever more efficient and effective neural pathways in the human brain:</u>

Toyota Production System (TPS) Founder Taichii Ohno said, "Without standards there can be no improvement." Figure 8 illustrates how standards are emphasized at every stage of problem solving. We compare our work to the standard to measure the gap between intention and actual performance (which reveals "mistakes" at the margin of competence). Standards are reinforced by two elements that provide a constant compass exposing gaps between current reality and True North:

1. A shared "True North" vision of the ideal level of TPS and
2. The "Toyota Way" business culture of mutual trust and respect.

- Repeatedly solving root causes of these "mistakes" produces *kaizen* (continuous improvement) for which Toyota is renowned.
- Hoshin (policy and objectives) is deployed down through the entire organization to the visual "Floor Management System," constantly revealing gaps between the desired ideal and the current actual (see Figure 7 in Hoshin Kanri section).
- Standardized Work "rules" and jidoka (machines and people stopping automatically when there is a problem) embedded in the culture make mistakes immediately visible for corrective problem solving.
- The culture demands that problems be exposed immediately. Work processes are designed to catch problems "in the moment." In a Toyota assembly plant this is once every 54 seconds, the time a vehicle takes to flow through a work station on the line, and the "andon cord" is pulled for help thousands of times a day, recovering quality and schedule <u>and</u> capturing facts and data on the problem for root-cause problem solving to prevent reoccurrence. People and machines stop when quality problems occur, which brings immediate attention and support—and another deep practice learning. How many times a day do your workers learn?

- Individuals and teams design their own work and do root-cause problem solving in order to improve processes and performance.
- Rather than telling subordinates what to do, leaders ask them questions that encourage them to exercise their brains by thinking about potential problems and causes ("20% direct/80% coach")

2. Department/Work Group: Process Management Continuous Improvement PDCA

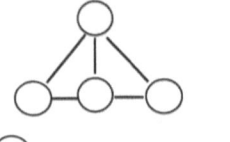

Group Members' Brains

Neural Pathways

Traditional organizations limit identification of dysfunctional interactions between team members. Examples:

- Company reward-and-recognition system encourages competition among colleagues for raises, bonuses, and promotions
- Competition between silo managers encourages loyalty to your manager and your silo as the way to get ahead
- Lack of clear understanding of next-process customer and end-customer requirements allows problems to be passed on unnoticed
- Lack of clear understanding of how job connects to the customer and the success of the business
- Emphasis on "doing" and "making my number" causes individuals to jump to a solution before fully understanding the problem, receiving input, and reaching consensus with other department members
- Expectations and "rules" for connections between manager and subordinate or between colleagues are unclear.

How Toyota facilitates effective and synergistic work and team learning:

- While individuals receive performance appraisals that influence career progression, pay raises and bonuses, Toyota places more emphasis on group and total company performance.
- Much greater effort using the scientific method goes into planning and building consensus before starting a project,

improving a process or implementing a solution to a problem. Working in teams provides a variety of perspectives and checks and balances—creating many cycles of deep practice that develop group capability. On-site observation of the problem or process (*genchi genbutsu*) facilitates full understanding of the problem and its impacts, and enables the observers to summarize facts and data so colleagues, stakeholders, supporting functions and management can contribute ideas to improve the solution and commit support.

- One of a Toyota manager's most important responsibilities is to develop his/her people. Problem solving—daily deep practice at the margin of competence—is the primary method for human and organizational development. Problem solving is presented visually on an A3-size (11" x 17") paper following the scientific method. The result is then presented for scrutiny, challenge, input and consensus from colleagues, stakeholders and management. This process—completed <u>before</u> the implementation of solutions—greatly strengthens both individual and group neural pathways.

3. <u>Extended Enterprise: Policy Management Continuous Improvement PDCA</u>

Now let's examine how the methods of "Deep Learning" described in *The Talent Code* can put your total organization on the path to greatness.

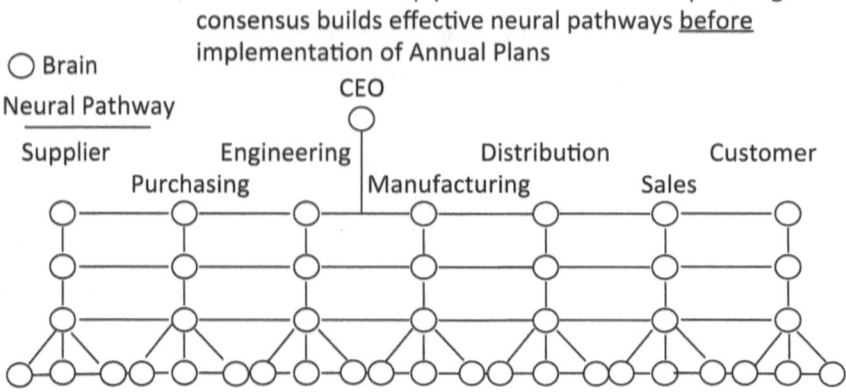

Examples of how traditional organizations limit frequent identification of mistakes in the interactions between enterprise functions along the horizontal flow of value to the customer, limiting the repetitive correction that grows myelin to make neural pathways faster, stronger and better synchronized:

- In a Management By Objectives (MBO) organization, "Strategy Deployment" often starts after budgeting and close to the start of the next year. Objectives are pushed from top management down through functional silos. Emphasis is on targets with much of the discussion focused on negotiating the target numbers rather than the means to achieve them—not much learning here.
- Functions independently plan their projects and actions to achieve their objectives. Consequently, when implementation begins conflicting priorities and projects compete for resources and support. Much of the year is wasted negotiating support and deciding actions, both of which should have been completed before the year began.
- Under pressure to achieve objectives, functional management often makes suboptimum decisions to achieve functional

objectives that hamper or prevent other functions from achieving their objectives—masking the mistakes in the function with the problem and generating symptoms of mistakes in the functions that are victims of the suboptimal decision—again no learning.
- Career paths within functions and "silo thinking" result in insufficient knowledge of the nature of work and problems in other functions—less cross-organizational collaboration and learning.
- All of the above combine to create few opportunities for identifying mistakes and solving problems in the connections between functions before the year's implementation of the planned projects. This is analogous to a football team's offensive line, receivers, running backs, defensive line and secondary independently drawing up and practicing their plays alone, and then going out to compete without practicing as a team.

<u>How Toyota facilitates enterprise-wide deep practice to grow ever more efficient and effective neural pathways along the connections between departments and functional divisions, breaching vertical silo walls with horizontal, enterprise-linking processes that create value for the customer</u>

- *Hoshin Kanri*: Four or five months before the start of the new year, management at every level begins to reflect with *hansei* on the current year's Annual Plan accomplishments versus plan, focusing on problem areas and causes. Based on the lessons learned, decisions are made about what future actions should be planned.

    o *Hansei* ("humble self-reflection") is essential to both individual and organizational learning and to the effective problem solving that fuels both. Without it, those challenged with solving a problem are far less effective. When I see below-expectation results and ask myself questions such as, "How have I failed . . . ?" and "What can I do better next time?" two things happen:

1. I see my mistakes, and I look at the situation more like a scientist formulating questions to guide my search for root causes that I can analyze to deduce facts and data to understand problem causes I can control or influence. In short, I learn. Contrast this with the "blaming" that occurs in most organizations. "I would have been successful, but I didn't get the support I needed from engineering." or "Severe weather prevented us from achieving our goal." or "The customers didn't understand our value proposition." This sort of behavior may get us off the hook with our boss and make us feel better, but it sure doesn't make us smarter or more successful.
2. *Hansei* also fosters respect from others whose support we need in a connected business system. Humility diffuses anger and engenders empathy. Pointing an accusatory finger has the opposite effect, alienating those we need to be successful and disabling the mutual trust, respect and collaboration essential in a Lean System Thinking organization

- When top management deploys the Company Annual Policy and Objectives, managers begin by identifying priorities and objectives for the new year. Horizontal coordination and collaboration between the managers across the functions (no longer silos) along the horizontal flow of value to customers develops consensus on Annual Plan actions to improve business processes in order to achieve targeted results. This horizontal planning and coordination provide deep practice that adds many layers of myelin, improving skills <u>and</u> making the neural pathways connecting people in various business processes faster, more effective and better synchronized. Additionally, a process the Japanese call "catchball" involves discussions between managers and their seniors about capability and challenges, enabling learning dialogues about alternatives, resources and support "We can achieve only a portion of our cost target here, but another manager has found an opportunity to make up the shortfall." All of this dramatically increases the organization's ability to successfully implement the resulting Annual Plan. Mid-Year and Year-End reviews provide PDCA, another myelin-layering activity.

- Toyota's corporate DNA creates an environment where the members of the entire company deeply practice the activities that make the neural pathways connecting people in various business processes faster, more effective and better synchronized. What are the values and beliefs that make this DNA so successful?

— Total focus on customer needs—both those of the <u>external</u> customer who buys a vehicle and those of <u>internal</u> customers in the next process.

— System thinking that makes each team member acutely aware that his actions positively or negatively impact other areas of the enterprise; this generates a commitment to cooperation that optimizes the total system.

— Highly developed PDCA problem-solving methodology using a Toyota-developed A3 report that makes the logic clearly visible so team members, stakeholders and management can challenge and improve the suggested solution. This "humble" reviewing develops consensus <u>before</u> implementation, which strengthens cooperation and makes the implementation go smoothly.

The Toyota Way provides no plateaus where employees can rest on their laurels after achieving current targets, because pausing would, of course, interrupt myelin creation. Renowned for its "permanent state of dissatisfaction," at Toyota to say "No problem" is a problem because a manager's job is to find problems and solve them ("deep practice"). When a manager has solved enough problems to consistently meet his KPIs, he must reduce resources or raise objectives to push back up to the "margin of competence where mistakes are repeatedly made and corrected" in order to continue the myelin-producing problem-solving process. <u>Continuous</u> improvement is mandatory.

If you want your people and your organization to be a gold medal-winning Olympic team serving customers better than your competition, you must provide opportunities for effective "deep practice" learning through PDCA problem-solving at every level:

- "In the moment" doing daily work, led by front-line management and supported by mid-level and top management
- In process improvements, led at the mid-level and supported from the top
- In strategic policy management business system design improvements led by top management

This ubiquitous deep practice learning will create strong, robust, effective, fast and synchronized neural pathways connecting all of the people and functions of your enterprise to execute your winning strategy at a level of exceptionalism never before experienced. Thanks to Daniel Coyle, we now have a deeper understanding of how Toyota's Lean System Thinking helps us do this.

AN OPPORTUNITY LOST

HOW AMERICAN BUSINESS GAVE AWAY A COMPETITIVE EDGE

The total quality control movement was started at the Bell Labs in America in the 1930s by Dr. Walter Shewhart, the founder of continuous improvement and mentor of the better-known Dr. W. Edwards Deming.

Shewhart defined the Plan-Do-Check-Act (PDCA) cycle, which he called the "Deming wheel" in honor of his most brilliant student. The quality-assurance methods created by Shewhart and Deming were adopted and used by American companies during the Second World War. But the companies saw no need for these rigorous methods after the war when pent-up demand and the destroyed factories of foreign competitors enabled them to sell everything they could produce regardless of quality. Because of this lack of interest, Deming and Joseph M. Juran, another Bell Labs expert, took the methods to Japan to support efforts by the U.S. Occupation Forces to help Japanese industry recover from the war's devastation.

Desperate Japanese companies embraced these proven methods. Dr. Yoji Akao incorporated the PDCA cycle into his work on Hoshin Kanri to create quantitative control points linked to company strategy, select metrics to check inputs to and performance of the processes that produce the targeted results, and monitor daily control activities to achieve each manager's annual plan of process improvement to increase capability. This is why Hoshin Kanri is often described as "results and means management."

Deming, Juran and the Japanese Union of Scientists and Engineers (JUSE) actively promoted the teaching of the methods in Japanese schools and their use in Japanese industry. Led by Dr. Shoichiro Toyoda, Toyota Motor Corporation so enthusiastically and effectively adopted the methods that it won JUSE's prestigious Deming Prize in 1965.

The abandoned Training Within Industry (TWI) curriculum, developed by the U.S. War Department during WWII, also was used by the U.S. Occupation Forces to revive Japanese industry. John Shook, Toyota's first American manager in Japan, rediscovered TWI when he was hired in 1981 to translate Toyota's production system and quality control training materials for the company's managers in America. One of his Japanese colleagues brought him the Japanese-language version of TWI. Shook read it and declared, "I don't think this will work in America."

The next day, his colleague brought him an English-language version. Shook was amazed to see that it was made in America and hadn't been changed by Toyota over the intervening 40 years since the War Department created it—an example of the automaker's amazing consistency and a reminder of the still-evident tendency of American business to overlook or undervalue obvious opportunities and threats.

The Fifth Input

How Business Can Use It to Save the American Dream

> "We need less government in business and
> more business in government."
> Warren G. Harding

Most business schools teach that companies combine four inputs—money, manpower, material and information—with planning, leadership, insight, innovation and several other ingredients to efficiently and effectively create value, which they sell to customers at a profit. Directing this process is called management. Because the laws of supply and demand that control our free market are inherently amoral, I tell my students to add a fifth input—*morality*—which requires them to have the courage to put others' interests before their own. An insufficiency of this vital fifth element in America's largest companies is driving the country toward disaster. Let me tell you how and why.

As business has become more global, complex, and competitive, both demand and compensation for top executives have grown—particularly in the United States. In 2008, the CEO's of 200 large American companies earned an average of about $7.6 million (including long-term incentives), nearly 300 times the pay of the average American worker. The gap between top and bottom closed to 263-1 in 2009, but rebounded to 325-1 in 2010 when average compensation climbed to nearly $11 million, despite a still tepid economy.[xxx]

According to the Hay Group, average European CEO pay typically totals $3-million to $4-million a year.[xxxi] Annual compensation for the average Japanese CEO is about $600,000—16 times the average Japanese worker's pay. Even Japan's largest company—Toyota Motor Corporation—paid President Akio Toyoda only about $1.4 million in 2011.[xxxii]

Here in America, executive compensation is a complex and socially explosive issue. Our founders ranked the right to work your way from poor to rich second only to freedom of religion. In fact, in his first draft of the Declaration of Independence Thomas Jefferson guaranteed the right to pursue "property", not "happiness." Our traditional admiration for alpha leaders out front on a horse and our practice of outrageously rewarding these "heroes" for their brilliance, skill, and leading-man vision also have helped mold our current executive compensation system. Allowing government to limit this right could start us down a slippery slope toward socialism and the eventual bankruptcy it usually yields.

To curb government's tendency to interfere, I believe prudent big-company executives should impose their own limits to avoid greed or the appearance of it. Instead, most allow their boards to overpay them and they hire armies of lawyers to lobby for tax breaks to further increase company earnings and their personal rewards. Here's a by-no-means-rare example.

In 2010, General Electric was America's 14th most profitable company with net global earnings of nearly $12 billion—including $5 billion here in the United States. Despite this positive result, Uncle Sam granted GE a $3.3-billion tax refund. Because of the excellent performance, the company's board paid CEO Jeff Immelt $15 million. Let me review: GE records huge earnings; GE's Board gives CEO Immelt a $15-million hug; American taxpayers get a $3-billion invoice. Meanwhile, cumulative profits held by 14 GE subsidiaries in Bermuda, Luxembourg and other tax havens climb by $10 billion. xxxiii

Although unwise, none of this is illegal and few companies would turn down a government refund. In fact, shareholders might sue if they did. But, not surprisingly, GE spent nearly $42 million on lobbying and political contributions in 2010—more than any other U.S. corporation—and Immelt was chairman of the President's Jobs Advisory Council, which Obama dissolved early in 2013 after only four meetings over two years.

Add layoffs to this sort of short-sighted, self-centered behavior and you create a really explosive mixture. In 2009, Hewlett-Packard paid then-CEO Mark Hurd $42 million for sharply increasing company productivity and earnings by laying off six thousand employees and cutting the salaries of the survivors by as much as 15%.xxxiv

Public reaction is predictable. In 2002, a research company called GlobeScan found that 80% of Americans considered our free-market system the world's best. By 2010, only 59% still did. Well-covered CEO pay had to be one of the factors driving this free fall in public respect for business. xxxv

Other surveys also show declining public support for capitalism and rising distrust of business. According to a recent study by the Institute for Policy Studies, 77% of Americans believe CEOs earn too much.xxxvi

Over time, continuous excessive pay for the top tier of American wage-earners is slowly creating a potential backlash of epic proportions. In 2011, the top one percent of U.S. wage-earners averaged more than $3.2-million of household income while the bottom 90 percent averaged about $31,000. The top $1/10^{th}$ of a percent averaged a staggering $27 million! Year by year, this disparity is accumulating into a growing wealth chasm. The constantly changing membership of the top one percent of U.S. households now possesses 33 percent of America's total wealth while the bottom 50 percent possesses less than 2 percent. Is it any wonder that Obama's anti-capitalist, soak-the-rich rhetoric won the election?xxxvii

Like a geological fault inching toward an inevitable earthquake, this ongoing accumulation is storing up social tension that will explode unless America's big companies help to decelerate and reverse the growing division between top and bottom.

Outside the U.S., the earthquake already has occurred and America is blamed as the epicenter. The 2008-09 financial meltdown pushed many countries to the edge of fiscal collapse and they view the recklessness and greed of American business as the primary cause. This has undermined the leadership value of the U.S. economic model and vaulted China much further up the global influence ladder.

The infusion of tax dollars into business during the meltdown provided government the perfect excuse to pander to resentment here and abroad by limiting executive pay in rescued U.S. companies. Now, as they try to recruit eventual successors, GM management is finding that the best and brightest tend to avoid bailed-out companies and their pay caps.

Meanwhile, regulatory compliance costs for American companies continue to explode as thousands of intrusive new rules flow out of Washington every year. When completely enacted, the 848-page Dodd-Frank financial control act will add thousands of new regulations to the Federal Register. The 2300 pages of the Affordable Healthcare Act—none of which Majority Leader Nancy Pelosi read before pushing it through the House of Representatives—will add thousands more and huge costs for taxpayers and companies. For example, the federally funded categories of illness and injury for which hospitals may claim reimbursement were scheduled to rise from 18,000 in 2012 to140,000 this year—including nine codes relating to injuries by parrots and three relating to burns from flaming water-skis![xxxviii]

The cost of business compliance with this often bizarre blizzard of governmental intrusion has been estimated to be as high as $1.75 trillion a year.[xxxix] Whatever the cost, it's a hidden tax companies pass on to consumers in the price of their goods and services. And much of it is self-inflicted. Companies invite intrusion with irresponsible behavior. And as economist Milton Friedman said, "Government can do anything with half the efficiency and twice the cost of the private sector." Not the sort of consultant you want giving you <u>mandatory</u> advice.

What other burdens does this torrent inflict on business and society?

- A substantial shift of jobs from satisfying customers to interpreting regulators and finding ways to game the ever-evolving system
- A stealthy government that buries unpopular taxes in regulatory mandates, forcing business to do what government itself does not want to be seen doing. Both routes (visible and invisible) drain the same source—the pocket of the taxpayer/consumer.

In the short term, big companies adapt to new regulations and pass on to consumers that portion of their compliance costs market conditions allow. In the long term, they slowly become less creative as government continues to slap their hands every time they reach for a new way of doing something. Small companies are simply crushed by a burden they lack the resources to handle.

Consider the misery and wreckage that could be avoided if the leaders of America's biggest companies would exercise more self-control and apply more of the fifth input to their management methods.

During my years in Washington, I met many ethical, effective, and admirable people who viewed public service as a duty. I also met many arrogant, self-centered ones who viewed it as an opportunity to gain recognition, garner wealth and gratify an overwhelming need to tell others how to live. They had forgotten that they derive their authority and resources "from the governed." Unfortunately, in government amnesia isn't a career-ending defect.

Once you let these forgetful people and the regulators swimming in their wake into your business, it is very difficult to dislodge them. Many of them long to replace the laws of supply and demand with a government-controlled nanny state where rewards are granted in return for obedience and support. And the longer they stay in Washington the stronger their arrogant confidence in their own wisdom becomes.

Why is this so dangerous? When Congress passes a law, the special interest groups (often including companies) that gave it life strive to sustain its government-conferred competitive advantage as long as possible. Business must stay lean, adaptive and reactive to survive in a continuously changing marketplace full of fierce competitors. But government is a monopoly with no competitors and no need to be efficient, effective or customer-oriented. That's why few politicians will rescind a law assuring a free flow of campaign funds even when the need for it has expired. Ronald Reagan called government programs "the nearest thing to eternal life on the planet."

The result is huge and growing government debt, regulatory overreach, and the long-term involvement of powerful people with sort-term viewpoints and little knowledge of or respect for the free market that has helped make America unique among nations. In their urgent haste to "fix" perceived problems and their unwarranted certainty that they can, they are likely to pile on enough cost, uncertainty and unintended consequences to permanently transform the United States from leader to laggard.

America's founders recognized that true value can be most abundantly created by free people laboring in a free economy where they are free to keep most of what they create. The fled Britain, fought a war, founded a nation, and forged a constitutional cage to—among other things—limit government interference with these value-creating activities. Unfortunately, over the past two centuries government has fought its way out of the cage.

When he left office after his second term as President, George Washington warned, "Like fire, government is a faithful servant, but a fearful master."[xl] Despite the obvious need to limit government growth and intrusion, many of America's biggest companies have instead crawled into bed with it, excusing their behavior with cynical sayings like, "If you're not at the table, you're on the menu."

There are nearly six million payroll-paying firms in the United States. Ninety-nine percent of them employ fewer than 500 people, providing jobs for nearly half our workforce.[xli] None of these smaller firms can afford the lobbyists the remaining 1% hire to seek competitive advantage in Washington. Nor can they avoid the torrent of regulations stirred up by their larger colleagues.

The members of this "1% Club" need to pull their noses out of the government feedlot long enough to focus on the shrinking economic horizon. While they trample on America's smaller companies to graze at the table of a dangerously out-of-control provider, anti-capitalist lions are creeping toward them through the long grass. They need to reunite with the 99% that contains many of their suppliers and customers to force government back into its cage. Why? Because all 100% of the business community and the entire country depend on the free-market system government is steadily eroding!

Businesspeople need to stand up and speak up for government action (or inaction) that expands economic opportunity as a whole rather than granting individual corporate feeding rights in return for obedient acceptance of ill-considered policies that often <u>dis</u>courage rather than <u>en</u>courage value creation. They need to demand that government actually cut budgets (not simply slow the rate of growth), freeze hiring, consolidate or eliminate agencies, write better laws that don't give civil-service bureaucrats so much interpretive room to create unintended consequences, and periodically review regulations so that private capital, <u>responsible</u> business behavior, and the self-regulating laws of supply and demand can once again unleash American power and productivity.

Regulation and a social safety net are absolutely necessary, but the pendulum has swung into an unaffordable twilight zone. Every day, the federal government "earns" more than $6 billion, spends more than $10 billion, and piles up debt like there is no tomorrow. [xlii]Government policies that confiscate and redistribute value without also supporting its creation are bound to fail. If you overtax and overregulate your only source of revenue (other than China, Japan and the U.S. Treasury's currency-printing presses), you will eventually bankrupt the private-sector wealth-creation that sustains America and—indirectly—the rest of the world.

Partisan, polarized politicians have no idea how to regain and sustain economic momentum. They are expert at rhetoric, regulation and redistribution, not restraint, and currently seem to create only gridlock, which prevents good politicians (of which there are some) from re-imposing sensible limits on government growth and interference. But it must be done!

Because I oversaw Toyota's government relations activities for 19 years and was a businessman for 35, I have some understanding of how difficult such a battle will be. The mainstream media, most of our public schools, many of our colleges and universities, our civil service, much of our judicial system, and at least half of Congress are dominated by those who want to grow government beyond necessary and affordable bounds in order to assure outcomes and exert control over private actions that is absolutely antithetical to our historical traditions. And they have been molding public opinion since Teddy Roosevelt was president.

That's why the attack on this long-standing conspiracy to deny America's birth rights must be generously funded, well-managed and persistent; all of which calls for leadership by the business community.

Most businesspeople would reply, "Impossible, you innocent fool!" They prefer to ride waves, not confront them. They also fear the 800-pound gorilla with the government-issued club and directors and shareholders who might question their judgment. And, of course, they don't want to curtail their rich rewards. This is the same short-sighted, greedy focus that gave away a made-in-America quality advantage after World War II.

Instead, businesspeople should take a long-term view and exercise the self-restraint and common sense that will allow them to retake the moral high ground from the politicians and regulators currently camped there.

Despite the risk-averse conservatism emphasized in this book, the biggest lesson I learned is that sometimes a little innocence is necessary. Big tasks present big risks and require big courage. If you always question the "how" before you commit to the "what" and take a leap of faith from the ledge, you will never achieve great things.

America's founders knew this. Two hundred and thirty-seven years ago in a little room of Philadelphia's Independence Hall, they dreamed a big dream and decided to defy the world's most powerful nation to make it come true. Business can and should help to rescue that dream for an America already waking up to the wrong tomorrow. If instead, America's biggest companies simply keep their noses buried in the government feedlot—rejecting reality, responsibility, and leadership for crumbs, contempt and presidential photo ops—the founders' dream and the exceptional nation it created will surely become—as Ronald Reagan once described the Soviet Union—"Just another failed experiment on the ash heap of history."[xliii]

Conclusion
And Key Lessons

- Management is the pursuit of excellence to delight customers and create profit and long-term value. In America, crucial byproducts of this pursuit have been national economic progress and a lifestyle other countries envy and attempt to emulate.
- Business transforms five inputs (money, manpower, material, information and *morality*) into one output: customer-defined value. If you do this efficiently, effectively, consistently, and creatively, customers will buy your output, funding you to continue delighting them.
- Over time, wealth—the lifeblood of new business—is created. Only human endeavor can create wealth; government can only *confiscate* wealth (by taxing), *borrow* it (by taking on debt future taxpayers will have to repay), or *redistribute* it from maker to taker.
- The basic tools and techniques to achieve business goals are conservative, ethical and practical. They change very slowly, if at all. At sustainably successful companies, the tools are embedded in an urgent, competitive, disciplined, "learning" culture constant at its core, adaptive at its margin, and based on skeptical, fact-based decision-making.
- Managers at these companies never waste a crisis. Instead, they recognize it as an opportunity to improve every aspect of their operations. They also know that success can breed complacency.

That's why they spend more time anticipating, analyzing and solving problems than celebrating victories or blaming each other for mistakes.
- They are very clear about company goals and relentless in pursuit of them. But they treat all stakeholders as business partners who deserve honest respect and a fair share of the value they help create.
- Nurturing and strengthening this sort of corporate culture requires smart, authentic, emotionally connected leaders who seek, learn, and teach—balancing principle with pragmatism and control with creativity.
- These leaders extract extraordinary performance from ordinary people by empowering, encouraging, coaching, supporting, rewarding, and holding them accountable.
- They and the successful companies they work for maintain a margin of safety; they continuously examine the world and evolve their plans and processes to stay in step with the changing environment; they continuously question basic assumptions, play the "what-if" game, prepare for potential disasters, and rarely overreach.
- They know that pride can create competitive spirit, but hubris lives next-door. They never take positive coverage of themselves or their company too seriously and they spend more time looking out the window than into the mirror.
- They relentlessly control cost, recycle waste, minimize structure and debt, and produce abundant results from non-abundant resources. They are disciplined, consistent, and extremely paranoid.
- If they must destroy formerly successful but now ineffective strategy and structure, they try to minimize the adverse impact on their workforce and apply the freed-up resources to new approaches more likely to succeed and benefit all stakeholders.

- They conserve resources during good times in order to—among other things—build competitive advantage during bad times.
- They do everything they can to assure the survival of the organization because without it there is no value-creation.
- When sacrifice is necessary, these leaders make certain it is shared fairly by all stakeholders, beginning with themselves, because they know that mutual success and sacrifice create *trust*—the mortar that binds these principles, practices, tools, and techniques into a successful whole.
- And they know deep within them that no enterprise—company or country—can succeed without roots and a constant productive culture.
- Although easy to understand, management is difficult and demanding to do and it includes dealing with many ongoing problems that have no ideal, final solution.

Without Trust, There Is No Bottom Line

At the heart of business is a transaction process that creates expectations. I loan you money because I believe you will pay me back. In fact, the words *creditor* and *credible* are based on the Latin word *credo,* which means "I believe." If you don't pay me back, I won't loan to you again. And if I sell you a product that doesn't fulfill your expectations, you won't buy from me again.

Without trust, this transparent transaction process cannot occur. Businesses that remember this and follow disciplined, conservative, trust-building practices generally succeed. Those that allow stupidity, cupidity, fad, arrogance or lassitude to steer them off-course generally fail.

My co-author and I are certain many clever, successful, cynical businesspeople would call our emphasis on core values, conservative practices, disciplined execution, and moral behavior unrealistic just as we would call their cynicism and greed short-sighted and inevitably destructive.

Instead of trading insults, let us reinforce our position with an observation from a much better-known business writer. Jim Collins wrote the best-selling management books *Built to Last, Good to Great, How the Mighty Fall,* and *Great by Choice.* In an interview with *Fortune* magazine, Collins had this to say about the importance of core values:

> "In times of great duress, tumult and uncertainty, you have to have moorings. Companies like P&G, GE, J&J, and IBM (*I would add Toyota*) have an incredible fabric of values, underlying ideals or principles that explain why it is important that they exist . . . The more challenged you are, the more you have to have your values. You need to preserve them consistently over time."[xliv]

> All we can add is *amen.*

A Glossary of Hoshin Kanri Terms, Tools and Techniques

- Hoshin Kanri: Japanese term for Strategy Deployment or Policy Deployment, which evolved as part of Total Quality Management. In Toyota, far more emphasis and time are spent collaborating and building consensus on highly defined Annual Plans and managing their successful completion on schedule.
- TQM or TQC: Total Quality Management or Total Quality Control is the application of the scientific method to every aspect of business to improve the delivery of value to customers. "Total" means that everyone in the organization is responsible for continuously improving the quality of processes, products and services. Toyota won the Deming Application Prize for TQC in 1965, and Total Quality remains an integral part of the company's DNA.
- Vision/Mission/Values/Strategy:

    o Vision: Description providing a visualization of the place and condition we want to be in the future.
    o Mission: Our purpose for being/existing. What we do to achieve our vision.
    o Values: Guiding principles and beliefs that guide our behaviors to create a business culture consistent with our Vision. Especially important to provide consistency, stability and psychological safety during periods of transformational change when new thinking and behaviors are needed.

o   Strategy: Our specific plans to define and achieve our business objectives:

— Mid-Range Plan: A 3-5 year plan identifying high-level priorities and objectives for the planning period. Meaningful organizational change that builds strategic competitive advantage cannot be achieved in one year. The Mid-Range Plan enables and encourages managers to tackle big improvements that often require investing a year or more in process improvement problem solving before benefits are realized. Short-sighted management focused on quarterly and annual earnings that impact stock price and bonuses need to adopt this longer-term thinking.

— Annual Policy and Objectives: Deployed at the beginning of each planning year to define how management should achieve results (policy), and quantitative targets/KPIs defining what to achieve (objectives). A proven and highly effective "policy" is "Apply Lean System Thinking to build strategic competitive advantage in . . . ."

— Annual Plan: Each manager's definition and documentation of his priority process improvement objectives to support top management's Annual Policy and Objectives. For each of the manager's objectives, he establishes a quantified target, assigns responsible person, prepares a detailed project implementation action plan, and identifies the departments whose support is needed to successfully implement the actions and achieve the targeted results. Up to three months are spent in "horizontal coordination" collaborating and negotiating to build consensus on coordinated plans and commitments to support each other.

— Annual Plan Management: Formal Mid-Year and Year-End Review Meetings where managers report Annual Plan progress, problems, and future corrective actions to Top Management. At lower levels of the organization, progress is checked and managed monthly and weekly—these are the highest priority projects in the company, and must be completed.

- A3 Report/Problem Solving using the Scientific Method: The Scientific Method is followed for all problem solving in Toyota. Often the problem solving process and results are reported on an "A3" (one 11" x 17" page). Like a scientist reporting his analysis of a perceived problem, the formation and testing of a hypothesis and final conclusions and applications of the learning, the A3 provides a clear and transparent flow of logic that enables the entire "scientific community" (i.e., colleagues, stakeholders and management in the company) to understand, contribute their ideas to improve the solution, align and support implementation, and apply the learnings elsewhere in the organization. A3s were developed uniquely in Toyota.
- Standard: A specification; a quantified target; a physical representation of acceptable vs. unacceptable (e.g., sample part, limit sample, photographs, engineering drawing); a clear definition of how work should be done (e.g., standardized work), requirements for products for information passed between processes, or definitions of flow paths and routing for products and information through the organization and between organizations. Standards enable (ideally "at a glance") the ability to see problems as a gap between normal and abnormal or ahead, on-time or behind. Continuous improvement requires continuous problem solving. Without standards, problems remain hidden. One of the most important roles for everyone in Toyota—especially managers—is to make problems visible.

- *Hansei*: Humble self-reflection (especially when seeing or experiencing a problem). *Hansei* is essential for members of a learning, continuously improving organization. When one asks, "What did I learn?" or "What can I do better next time?" one learns. He also gets more empathy and support from others to solve the problem. When one points the finger of blame at someone else or something else, he may feel better, but does not learn. When a subordinate does not perform or act in the way expected and the leader's first question is, "How have I failed to help them understand?" or ". . . to provide the necessary tools, working equipment and training needed?" more problem solving and continuous improvement occurs. This is a big part of the "mutual trust and respect" in the Toyota culture.
- Sustaining and starting with 5S: One of the biggest challenges and disappointments for organizations new to Lean or any process improvement methodology is sustaining the improvements after they are implemented. The primary reason is that they have not yet developed the self-correcting mechanisms to effectively solve the many disrupting problems that occur every day in any organization which are amplified in impact after improvement changes are made. In complex business processes, many problems are not easily visible, so creating the needed capability is difficult.

This is why starting with 5S is valuable—DONE THE TOYOTA WAY—with *hansei*, with a high priority on making problems visible, with a "Do it now!" sense of urgency for action to solve problems, with servant leadership from management and the extra resources and expertise needed at the beginning to do it "right from the start."

5S is the name of a workplace organization method that uses five phases: sorting (removing what is not needed), set in order ("a place for every thing, every thing in its place"), systematic cleaning (dirt and clutter hide problems), standardizing (making the "rules" clear and binary), and sustaining (always the hardest part) that describe how to organize a work space for efficiency and effectiveness by identifying and storing the items used, maintaining the area and items, and sustaining the new order. Almost everyone understands how 5S improves the appearance, safety, efficiency and effectiveness of the worksite and morale of the employees. Unfortunately, most also think 5S is something you do once, and then set up an audit program to maintain it (and watch it deteriorate). And then before an important visitor comes, get serious and clean up again—like it's all for show! (This is a lot like the workbench in my garage.)

By its very nature, 5S is visual. For example, tools are taken out of tool boxes or from shelves under work benches and placed on a shadow board (the place where each tool hangs has a painted silhouette in the shape of the tool). Anyone can see at a glance when the 5/16" wrench is not where it belongs, so the problem is clearly visible. The problem should be highlighted immediately and information gathered for problem solving. As soon as possible, the problem should be solved, by the team, with the support, guidance and coaching of their boss, with the support and coaching of the boss' boss. The problem should be solved to root cause so it does not happen again. The culture should evolve until the wrench is always returned to the proper place because "that is the way the game is played"—just like the youngster first learning to play baseball runs to first base after he hits the ball.

Your business is big and complex, with many moving parts, often scattered over a wide geography, and other challenges in managing both the visible and invisible processes and problems. If you cannot create a problem solving culture that can solve the problem of the wrench not being in the proper location on the shadow board, how do you expect your organization to solve the problems that cause other process improvements to deteriorate?

Start small with a "narrow and deep" pilot, and—with *hansei*—learn what management must do to create your sustaining continuous improvement culture.

Books That Provided Illumination

- *Are the Rich Necessary?* by Hunter Lewis
- *Contemporary Management* by Gareth Jones and Jennifer George
- *Management Rewired* by Charles Jacobs
- *Product Development for the Lean Enterprise* by Jeffrey Liker, Jim Morgan and Michael Kennedy
- *Toyota Culture: The Heart and Soul of the Toyota Way* by Jeffrey Liker and Mike Hoseus
- *Better Capitalism* by Robert Litan and Carl Schramm
- *How Markets Fail* by John Cassidy
- *Moral Intelligence* by Doug Lennick and Fred Kiel
- *Setting the Table* by Danny Meyer
- *The Talent Code* by Daniel Coyle
- *The Essential Wooden* and *Wooden: a Lifetime of Observations and Reflections On and Off the Court* by John Wooden and Steve Jamison
- *Ike: an American Hero* by Michael Korda
- *Killer Angels* by Michael Shaara
- *Joshua Chamberlain: the Soldier and the Man* by Edward G. Longacre
- *On the Art of War* by Sun Tzu
- *The Fifth Discipline* by Peter M. Senge
- *Great By Choice* by Jim Collins and Morton T. Hansen
- *Who's the Fairest of Them All* by Stephen Moore

End Notes

i	The Yale Book of Quotations
ii	Wikipedia
iii	Contemporary Management by Jones and George
iv	Contemporary Management by Jones and George
v	Wikipedia
vi	Wikipedia
vii	Brainyquote.com
viii	Dow Jones Industrials website
ix	Fortune 5-5-08
x	Wikipedia
xi	Wikipedia
xii	Personal experience
xiii	The Three Musketeers by Alexandre Dumas
xiv	The Economist 6-25-09
xv	Wikipedia
xvi	Wikipedia
xvii	Setting the Table by Danny Meyer
xviii	Wikipedia
xix	Fortune 4-13-10
xx	Ike: An American Hero by Michael Korda
xxi	The Yale Book of Quotations
xxii	The Essential Wooden by John Wooden and Steve Jamison
xxiii	Business Week 9-29-08
xxiv	Wall Street Journal 8-10-07
xxv	Wall Street Journal 7-08-07

xxvi The Fifth Discipline: The Art and Practice of Learning Organizations by Peter M. Senge
xxvii What Is Total Quality Control? by Kaoru Ishikawa
xxviii Wikipedia
xxix The Talent Code: Greatness Isn't Born, It's Grown by Daniel Coyle
xxx Associated Press-A&P 500 Compensation Survey; U.S. Department of Labor; Executive Excess 2011 by the Institute for Policy Studies
xxxi Wall Street Journal/Hay Group 2011 Compensation Study
xxxii Japanese CEA Compensation by Think Progress; Toyota 2011 annual report
xxxiii Executive Excess 2011
xxxiv Business Week 6-8-09
xxxv GlobeScan 2010 Survey of Public Attitudes
xxxvi Executive Excess 2011
xxxvii Historical Net Worth & Wealth Concentration in the United States by Jagg Xaxx; Facts on Concentration of Wealth by George Draffan; U.S. Census Bureau
xxxviii Ten Thousand Commandments 2011 by Clyde Wayne Crews Jr.; Heritage Foundation backgrounder 2663/3-13-12; The Economist 2-18-12
xxxix Ten Thousand Commandments
xl Wikipedia
xli U.S. Census Bureau
xlii Federal Government Revenue Vs. Spending 1947-2012 by ITO
xliii Wikipedia
xliv Fortune 4-13-10

www.ingramcontent.com/pod-product-compliance
Lightning Source LLC
Chambersburg PA
CBHW032018170526
45157CB00002B/755